The Coming of Saska

Also by Doreen Tovey
and published by Bantam Books

CATS IN MAY
CATS IN THE BELFRY
DOUBLE TROUBLE
THE NEW BOY
MORE CATS IN THE BELFRY

The Coming
of Saska

Doreen Tovey

BANTAM BOOKS

LONDON · NEW YORK · TORONTO · SYDNEY · AUCKLAND

THE COMING OF SASKA
A BANTAM BOOK : 0 553 40744 9

First publication in Great Britain

PRINTING HISTORY
Bantam edition published 1995

Set in 12/15pt Linotype New Baskerville
by Phoenix Typesetting, Ilkley, West Yorkshire.

Bantam Books are published by Transworld Publishers Ltd,
61–63 Uxbridge Road, Ealing, London W5 5SA,
in Australia by Transworld Publishers (Australia) Pty Ltd,
15–25 Helles Avenue, Moorebank, NSW 2170,
and in New Zealand by Transworld Publishers (NZ) Ltd,
3 William Pickering Drive, Albany, Auckland.

Reproduced, printed and bound in Great Britain by
Cox & Wyman Ltd, Reading, Berks.

Chapter One

When I told Father Adams we were planning another trip to the Rockies – to do some more riding, I said, and look for the grizzlies we'd missed last time, and if possible see something of the wolves – he looked at me as if I needed certifying.

He usually does look at me like that, of course. Charles and I have lived along the lane from him for more than eighteen years now, but in his eyes we are still essentially townsfolk and therefore dim beyond redemption when it comes to the commonsense matters of life.

This time, however, he regarded me even more old-fashionedly than usual. 'Hassn't thee got enough wild animals round here?' he said. And then, in a voice deep with concern because really he is rather fond of us, 'Thee'st want to watch thee dussn't get *et.*'

I knew what he was thinking of. For one thing the previous week, when we'd been bringing down logs from our two and a half acres of woodland, which is across the lane from the cottage. It could almost have been a scene from the Canadian backwoods then, with Charles stacking the logs at the road-edge and me loading them on to a roughly constructed sledge so that Annabel, our donkey, could haul them down to the cottage.

The idea of the sledge was because the hill is so steep. With wheels the load of logs would probably have shot straight to the bottom with Annabel on top – but with runners it slid gently down behind her, the weight acting as a brake, and it towed up easily again when empty.

Annabel loved it. Not wanting to overburden her . . . she is, after all, only a very small donkey . . . at first I'd tied just a couple of logs to the sledge. She'd wafted them down to the valley as if they were balloons, so next time I'd added a couple more . . . and the time after that another two . . . until eventually she was pulling quite a load on every trip. Enjoying it, too. Plodding down the hill with the air of an experienced, if pint-sized, dray-horse and the complacently smug expression on her face that Charles and I knew only too well.

She stood patiently at the bottom while I unloaded the logs on to the grass verge outside the cottage; pulled the sledge back up again without even the slightest pause (normally I'd have to haul her up it bodily, with her fighting to eat dandelions at every step); stood again at the top while I re-loaded . . . 'I wish we had a camera handy,' I said to Charles as, with me walking at her head, she started down the hill once more. 'Or that somebody would come along and see her. Nobody ever *does* when she's being good like this.'

That did it. Mention the word 'good' in Annabel's hearing and, it being her lifelong principle to be the opposite, non-co-operation sets in at the speed of sound. At the end of that descent she decided she'd had enough of playing at draught horses. Unfortunately I had my foot on the sledge-rope at the time, anchoring it while I unloaded the logs, so when she moved off down the other fork of the lane (away, that is, from any direction that could possibly be connected with log-hauling), she not only took the still half-loaded sledge with her but me as well, sliding along behind it on my bottom with my foot caught in the rope.

Overburden her, did I say? The sledge and I went down the lane behind her as if we were so much balsa wood. The lane leads, if one follows it far enough, to the field of a donkey friend of hers called Charlie, some three miles away, and I'd no doubt have gone the whole way to Charlie's on my seat if it hadn't been that Father Adams happened to be a short way down there clearing a blockage in the stream at the time, and Annabel shied and stopped when she saw his head come up out of the ditch.

I scrambled up, grabbed her bridle and explained what had happened. Father Adams said nothing for a moment. Just looked at me resignedly from under his hat brim. 'Wur's the Boss?' he asked at length. When I explained that Charles was still up at the top of the hill bringing logs out to the road-edge . . . *I had* shouted but he couldn't have heard me above the noise of the stream, I said, and anyway he was singing when I left . . . that didn't help things either. Charles has a very good voice, but his habit of singing when working among his fruit trees is down on Father Adams's scorecard as another of our peculiarities.

I remember on one occasion Charles rendering 'On Yonder Hill Declining' from *Fra Diavolo* . . . standing on a slope in the orchard, one arm out-thrown in the manner of Gigli, performing, as he thought, entirely for my benefit . . . and in the pause after a ringing 'Dia . . . vo . . . lo . . . o prou . . . oud . . . ly stands' a familiar voice floated up from the lane, 'Ah, an' if he done a bit more weedin' instead of standin', maybe we could see the trees for the nettles.'

No. Years of being our nearest neighbour and therefore rarely missing a thing we do has done nothing to alter Father Adams's conviction that what we need is a keeper. If I couldn't cope with a donkey hauling logs, I could see him thinking, what chance would I have against a grizzly?

We couldn't even win with Siamese cats. We had two. Seeley, a four-year-old seal-point and Shebalu, a two-year-old blue-point. And if evidence was needed of our ineptitude in that direction there was, to take the latest example, the affair of Seeley and the dog-food.

This had come about as the result of the husband of Shebalu's breeder calling to see us one day when he was on business in our neighbourhood. 'Good Lord, hasn't she grown!' he said, hardly able to believe that the tall, beautiful, serenely elegant blue-point who swayed top-model fashion across the room to greet him was the same matchstick-tailed little scrap who used to race up and down his curtains. 'She's twice the size of her mother.'

'It's the country air,' I told him. 'And tearing about the hillside. And of course she eats like a horse.' At which we got to talking about feeding – pigs' hearts and lean mince they liked, I said, and didn't it cost a bomb . . . tinned food was good and cheaper, but we couldn't get them to eat much of it . . . and he said Shebalu's mother didn't like tinned cat-food either, but now they fed her on Chum. She and their dog side by side, from twin bowls, and she ate it as though it were caviare.

Aha! I thought. The next time I went to the village shop I too brought home some Chum. Shebalu was the real stumbling block when it came to the tinned cat-food business. Seeley, our amiable gannet, would eat it if he had to. It was just that it didn't seem fair to feed him on tinned stuff while Shebalu held out for fresh meat. If her mother liked dog-food, however, perhaps she would, too, and that would solve the problem. Not only as regards cost. Our Vet had told us years before that cats *should* eat a fair proportion of tinned pet food. It was scientifically balanced, he said – particularly the kind that contained cereal – and cats were much less likely to get kidney trouble in later life if their diet wasn't exclusively meat and fish.

So I got the Chum. Shebalu refused to look at it, saying she didn't care what her mother said. What jurisdiction did She have, anyway, letting her Daughter leave home at Eight Weeks Old, bawled Abandoned Annie indignantly at the very thought of it. Seeley tunnelled into it saying it was super . . . better than rabbit, he assured us between noisily appreciative slurps. How were we to know that, having eaten his and Shebalu's platefuls and presumably seen the picture on the tin, his Siamese mind would translate that into meaning that *he* was now a dog, so from now on he was going to behave like one?

He started that very afternoon. When I opened the back door to take them out for their four o'clock run, there, on the other side of it, was one of our neighbours about to put the church news-sheet through our letterbox. Behind her was her dog, a huge black muscle-rippling Labrador at the sight of whom Seeley would normally have fled indoors and hidden under the table.

What, fortified by Chum, did he do on this occasion? Stick his neck out, growl like a guard dog, and charge. 'Seeley!' I screeched, diving after him. 'Bramble!' yelled the woman, making a futile grab at her dog. Round the corner of the cottage we tore, expecting to find Seeley demolished on the lawn – and what incredible scene met our eyes?

Bramble sitting down hard on the front path, presumably to stop himself from running away, shivering like a jelly with his ears flat in surrender . . . and, stalking intimidatingly towards him like Gary Cooper in *High Noon*, our normally timid little Seeley.

I grabbed him, wondering what he might do to me in that mood, but he knew even then that I was his friend. He let me carry him away, his coat bushed out like a porcupine, contenting himself with shouting threats over my shoulder as he went. Show his nose in our Valley again and he'd have his Ears off, he bawled at the terrified Bramble. Set foot on our Path and he'd Eat Him. Wet Just Once More on our gatepost and he'd . . . what dreadful Siamese retribution that would incur we didn't hear. By that time I'd dumped him in the conservatory and locked the door.

I apologized to our neighbour saying it must have been the dog-food and she said she reckoned the Rector should pay her danger money . . . both of us laughing, seeing that nobody had been hurt, and neither of us serious in what we said . . . and a week later Seeley did it again.

This time he'd been up on the hillside in the Forestry Commission estate with me and Shebalu. Basking in the late afternoon sunshine, hunting in the bracken for mice, the pair of them chasing each other up the fir trees . . . Shebalu shinning effortlessly up like a stevedore mounting the Eiffel Tower; Seeley, like Solomon before him, achieving four feet up with an excited yell to Look At Him and then falling off with a plop. They'd had their fun and were back sitting on the rug with me when

a man leading a horse and accompanied by a boy and an Alsatian dog appeared in the lane below us.

Normally – this, for safety's sake, was something I'd taught them long ago – when we saw a dog the three of us vanished silently into the undergrowth. A right nit I felt too, at times, crouched in a clump of bracken peering out with a couple of cats, but I thought it was good to set an example.

This time, however, before I could make a move, Seeley was up and streaking downhill to the attack. True when he reached the bottom and the Alsatian barked at him he lost his nerve and dodged into an old stone ruin; just over the Forestry fence, it had always been a refuge for our cats. But no sooner did the bitch turn away, called off by the man who said she wouldn't harm him, she was young and only playing, than Seeley shot out again like a cannon ball, thinking her retreat meant that she was afraid of *him*.

By this time, actually, she was. Back to her owner she fled, with Seeley like an avenging fury at her heels. Up in the air went the horse – thank goodness the man wasn't riding him. How I managed to field Seeley as he passed me I will never know. Only that somehow, as in a dream, I did – reflex action is second nature to the owners of Siamese cats – and that I was dimly aware in the background of the man hanging on to the rearing horse, the boy getting up on the bank for safety, Charles running like mad down from the orchard – and, watching

from the lower lane, registered even in my extremis
by the downturned brim of his trilby, the silent,
Job-like figure of Father Adams.

Sometimes I wonder how he does it. Fell a tree up
in the top hedge of our wood and round the corner
as it falls will come Father Adams. Not deliberately,
because he's heard the sawing and wants to know
who it is, but because he's happened to come that way
home from the pub. Get out quietly repairing one of
our garden walls – they are dry-stone walls and always
tumbling down – and, just as one puts on a wrongly-
balanced stone and the whole lot falls down again,
there on the other side of it will be Father Adams.

It was a foregone conclusion, therefore, that he'd
be in at the end of the dog-food experiment. It was a
few days later and we'd stopped giving Seeley Chum.
Another Siamese owner had told us that her Vet said
one shouldn't feed cats on dog-food. Different types
of animals have different metabolisms, she said, and
the foods are geared specially to their needs.

We did rather wonder – while telling ourselves
that the dog-chasing was, of course, just coincidence
– whether leaving it off would make a difference in
that respect. Even we didn't bargain for anything so
spectacular, however, as that on Wednesday there
was Seeley chasing an Alsatian and by Sunday, sans
the Chum, we were back to dogs chasing *him*.

'Whass he doin' up there?' asked Father Adams,
appearing as if by press-button as we once more
hoisted our extension ladder against an ash-tree some

fifty yards down the lane. Down through the leaves, from the topmost branch, peered two blue eyes round with woe. Like Solomon before him, while normally a non-climber, when danger threatened he could get up all right; the snag was, also like Solomon, that he then developed vertigo and couldn't get down.

'Don't tell I he've chased a dog up *there,*' went on Father Adams, ready after eighteen years to believe anything as far as our animals were concerned. Anything, that is, except the truth. That Seeley had fled up there at the sight of a passing Corgi and didn't Father Adams think it queer, I said, that he'd chased dogs when we gave him dog-food and got chased by them when we didn't?

'Sometimes it strikes I thee bist,' said our neighbour, who is a man of few but succinct words. In the circumstances it was hardly surprising that he worried about us meeting up with grizzlies.

Chapter Two

Normally Miss Wellington would have worried too. She was always worrying about other people. Whether somebody ought to be told about the way they kept their garden. (Miss Wellington's, where it could be seen for the stone gnomes and toadstools that dotted it like the Bayeux Tapestry, was immaculate and couldn't be faulted.) Whether Annabel was happy. Miss Wellington spent many an anxious hour pondering this at Annabel's fence and, because Annabel always bawled when she moved away, was sure she needed a companion. Annabel was actually informing the world that Miss Wellington was stingy with the peppermints . . . we could always tell her disgusted calls by the derisive snort at the end. But Miss Wellington liked to worry. It made life so much more interesting.

She worried about the church heating. She worried about what things were coming to. She worried considerably about the young people of today. She'd done that ever since she saw their goings-on on television and now – which was why she wasn't as yet at hysteria stations at the thought of us going out to look for grizzlies – she had a trendy young couple living next door to her and she was worrying more than ever.

Convinced that all young men with beards had sinister motives and that flowing dresses and beads were a sign of fecklessness in girls, Miss Wellington nearly dropped when she saw the Bannetts looking over Rose Cottage. Ern Biggs, Father Adams's rival for the handyman jobs in the village, was working in a nearby garden at the time and according to him she went straight indoors and started playing hymns on her piano. 'Oh God Our Help In Ages Past,' he said, and whether it was to frighten them off or in the hope of invoking heavenly protection nobody knew, but either way it didn't work. The Bannetts bought the cottage, Miss Wellington fluttered round the village anticipating the worst – the place taken over by hippies and probably a pop festival on the village green before we'd finished . . . and the week before they moved in, everybody had a fright.

Everybody except us, that is. We happened to be coming back from town around ten o'clock at night and while, as we turned the corner by the Rose and Crown and drove along the lane, we were startled ourselves for a moment to see Rose Cottage apparently floodlit, with music throbbing out from it like Congo drums, we did get the true picture as we passed.

The Bannetts were showing another couple around (Liz Bannett's parents, it later transpired). The *son et lumière* effect was the result of their having switched on the high-powered lamps installed by the builders for working on the dark, low-ceilinged interior. During the day, when the builders were using them, the lights didn't show up so much; at night, through the uncurtained windows, they shone out like the Eddystone lighthouse. The music, we further realized as we drove slowly past with the car windows down (being as interested in our neighbours as anybody), was Beethoven . . . probably there was a concert on the radio . . . and it could be heard so clearly because the cottage door was open: the Bannetts and their visitors were just leaving and Tim Bannett was turning off the lights.

That wasn't how the story hit the village, though. 'Wunt half a party up at Rose Cottage last night,' Father Adams told us when he brought us in some leeks. 'Place all lit up like a gin palace,' said Fred Ferry when I met him in the lane. The Rose and Crown was the nearest he'd ever been to a gin palace but Fred likes a dramatic turn of phrase. 'People up there drinkin' and carryin' on,' Ern informed everybody he met. This was his interpretation of Fred's gin palace, of course. Ern lives in the next village himself and hadn't personally witnessed anything.

If Miss Wellington had heard the Beethoven she might have been happier about her prospective neighbours. Miss Wellington is a great believer in culture. But she happened to be away visiting her brother for a couple of days and was told the tale, on her return, by Father Adams. Supported by Fred

Ferry and Ern Biggs, of course, who were at her gate as fast as their boots would carry them. We were very kind, she told us when we tried to give her our version of the affair. She realized we were trying to spare her. She knew as well as we did what modern young people were like, however. She'd never be surprised at anything that happened.

Miss Wellington was always expecting things to happen. Only recently one of our neighbours had had his car banged in the lane near the church, by somebody coming round the corner on the wrong side. Miss Wellington's comment on this had been that it wasn't safe to go out these days without taking a bath and when I asked what that had to do with it – 'In case one were hurt and taken to hospital,' said Miss W. 'One wouldn't want to go there dirty, would one?'

What with presumably taking baths and waiting for the next-door orgies to start, Miss Wellington was pretty busy that summer. She was conspicuous by her absence from the preparations for our safari, anyway, which was probably just as well. It would only have needed her at her usual rate of attendance and we'd have gone clean up the wall.

There was so much to do, and so many people to tell us how to do it. For a start there was the garage door to be repaired. One of a pair of doors actually, made of heavy metal sheeting on wooden frames, and over the years one of the doorposts had rotted, and the door on that side had sagged

and was dragged nightly into position by Charles
with a horrible shrieking noise, and Father Adams
had been saying for months that if we didn't put
he right we'd have a fine old job on there, and
now of course we had. Not only was the door off
its hinges at the top, but with all the dragging, the
metal sheeting was adrift from its frame, bent into
the bargain, and Charles was saying we couldn't go
to Canada and leave the door like that.

I couldn't see why not. We left it like that every
time we went out, propped up with a spade so it
wouldn't fall down, and nobody had tampered with
it yet. It contained, in any case, only our old car, our
sixteen-foot canoe (either of which would have been
spotted by the neighbours to a man if it had gone up
the hill with anybody else) and a load of old junk that
nobody but Charles could find a use for. Even he, I
sometimes doubted, would hardly find a use for the
picture of his Aunt Ethel as a girl clutching a tennis
racket, or a stepladder minus its steps.

Charles thought otherwise, however, so there he
was for about a fortnight, putting in a new doorpost,
hammering the metal sheeting flat, making a complete new frame for the back of the door . . . every
morning laying the whole thing on the driveway for
easy working and every night hoisting it back to fill
the gap again.

Our mentors were in their element, of course.
'Told thee theest should have done he months ago,'
Father Adams advised us a dozen times a day. 'Still

workin' on thee raft then?' was Fred Ferry's daily
quip about how we were going to Canada. 'Theest
do better to let I finish he,' Ern Biggs said hopefully
and persistently – to which Father Adams's reply was
that finished it certainly would be if Ern Biggs ever
laid hammer to it.

Finished it eventually was, though – perfectly, as
Charles does everything, though it takes him a time in
the doing of it. And then he painted it, still flat on the
drive for convenience and, as the paint wasn't dry, for
the first time ever we didn't hoist it into the gap that
night and the next morning we found we had visitors.

We'd noticed them the previous evening. Two
exhausted swallows resting on our telephone wire
after their thousand-mile flight from Africa: a sign
that summer had come. 'Young ones,' said Charles.
'Probably born up at the farm last year.' And then,
after marvelling at the tremendous distance they'd
flown and the instinct that brought them back to
raise their own young in this remote corner of
England where they themselves had been born,
we thought no more about it. They were just
resting. They wouldn't stay with us. We'd never
had swallows in the Valley. At the farm at the
top of the hill, yes – they'd nested in the barn up
there for years. But the only comparable structure
in the Valley was Annabel's stable and obviously
the roof of that wasn't high enough for them.

Except that now there was our garage with its door
off, on the very evening the swallows arrived . . .

and there was this young pair (they reminded him
of the Bannetts, said Charles) obviously wanting to
set up on their own . . . though how they could
have known our garage door was off, nearly half a
mile away from the barn . . .

They were still there next morning, perched on the
wire, considering the space where the door should
have been and occasionally venturing through it.
They watched everything that happened during the
day. The cats going up to the vegetable garden to
eat grass, Annabel being led out of her stable and
put up on the hill, Charles putting a second coat of
paint on the recumbent door . . . careful to avoid
appearing to notice them but they were certainly
studying him, he said. Several times the male had
swooped daringly low over his head while the female,
much more cautious, twittered anxiously, like Miss
Wellington, from the wire.

They moved in, of course. Who wouldn't with those
high rafters waiting to be nested in, mud for building
in the stream bank by the garden wall, a valley full
of insects for the catching and a couple of humans
who, having been deliberately tested, obviously didn't
object to swallows?

There was no question of our putting back the
garage door. There it stood, propped against the wall,
while Father Adams said we were never right, Fred
Ferry told everybody we couldn't rehang it because
it didn't fit, and the swallows swept confidently in
and out. 'What be goin' to do when theest go to

Canada?' asked Ern. Charles said the brood would be flying by then.

They were flying all right. We watched through the weeks – when we should have been doing so many other things – while the nest was built, like a tiny parson's pulpit, high under the roof, snug against a rafter: while the eggs were laid, and then hatched – there were four of them and the cleverness of the nesting site was revealed. They'd chosen the one rafter that adjoined a bracing strut that ran right across the garage and there, when they were hatched, four little swallows were able to sidle out, even before they could fly, sit in a row as on a trapeze bar, and peer out at what went on in the garden. What was more, said Charles, if they did fall they'd land in the canoe, which was suspended by ropes from the roof. Wasn't that clever of the parents?

It certainly was, though we didn't appreciate it quite so much when we got the canoe down one afternoon to do a bit of practice on the river and saw what they'd done to the inside. Four little swallows sitting up there getting excited . . . still, as Charles said, at least it kept it off the car.

Where, you may ask, were the cats while all this was going on? In the canoe themselves, if they got the chance. They would get on the car roof, from there up into the canoe, and sit there one in each seat section. They couldn't reach the swallows, who knew it perfectly well and took no notice of them. We didn't bother either – for once we knew where

the pair of them were – but it certainly shook Ern Biggs when he saw them. He'd called to ask if we wanted any work done. I sent him up to see Charles, who was in the garage, and he'd looked up when he heard the swallows twittering. 'N there were thic cats,' he reported later in the Rose and Crown, 'sittin' up in thic canoe, like a couple of they Polynesian Islanders.' He'd apparently added that, knowing us, it wouldn't have surprised he if they'd paddled the ruddy thing out of the garage.

We soldiered on. We couldn't put the door back but there were plenty of other things to be done. Getting the garden straight; studying maps and getting our luggage together; me practising up on my riding.

For me this was a necessity. Among other things we were going to revisit our friends on a couple of Alberta ranches and while I knew full well that Charles, as had happened last time, would go out there not having ridden for ages, leap into a Western saddle and go careering about the range as if he'd been born on it, I also knew that I, who never missed a week without riding in England, didn't have Charles's way with horses whatsoever.

On our last visit I'd been lent, on one ranch, a fat little cow-pony called Sheba who was adept at slipping her saddle. True I'd had to concentrate on riding lop-sidedly – to get her saddle back straight every time she slipped it sideways because I hadn't a clue as to how to tighten a cinch. But that should have been all in a day's work. I shouldn't, as both she and I knew was the case, have been in danger of vanishing over the horizon if for a moment I let her have her head.

This time, I decided, it would be different. I too would manage my horse, like Charles, by the way I sat it and used my legs. I too would ride nonchalantly, reins in one hand, with my mount moving obediently beneath me. To which end I was practising diligently at the local stables, supervised by Mrs Hutchings and her daughter.

As always I rode Mio, the Number Two horse of the remuda. Merlin was still there – twenty years old now, the grand old man of the stables and still the best bet on which to mount beginners: carrying them carefully as babies until he knew they had their balance, then cantering with them regardless – though still gently – just to prove to them that they could go. So was Cobnut, the fast little dark chestnut gelding beloved of my friend Tina, who was a nurse. So were Gusto who, with me clinging to his neck, had once given a Wild West bucking demonstration, and Kelly, the eternally doleful Irish horse, and Alex, the big chestnut hunter.

Of the others, Halberdier was now retired, Zaboine had been bought by his favourite rider and gone to live with him on Exmoor – and Jasper, the tall black thoroughbred, was dead.

Tragedy had struck once more, as it can so easily with thoroughbreds. Jasper had developed leg trouble, which had been diagnosed as chronic arthritis. He'd had supports, injections, lengthy, expensive treatment . . . Lynn Hutchings, who'd trained him from a yearling, had nursed him like a baby. It was no use. At first there were intervals when his leg appeared to be normal – and then, for no apparent reason, he would be limping, in pain again. If he was kept in his box, his leg improved to a degree but he became bad-tempered with frustration. If he was put out to grass, even on his own, he would try to gallop because that, for him, was what life was for – and his leg would go again. Towards the end, while the Vet tried a last desperate treatment to save him, he lived permanently in his box. It was heartbreaking to see him watching as the other horses went out on a ride. Gusto, who'd been his grazing companion in happier days on the hill. Mio, with whom he'd loved to race. And then Jasper, whose joy it had been to skim across the Downs as if on wings, would come out for his own exercise and limp painfully around the yard.

The treatment failed. There was nothing more to be done, said the Vet . . . and sadly the Hutchings agreed. There was no question of retiring him like Halberdier. He would have been in pain for the rest of his life. So now Jasper was gone, at only seven years old, and in his place was Kestrel: a fine-tempered chestnut thoroughbred who looked very like Zaboine. There was also, which complicated things considerably, another newcomer called Barbary.

Chapter Three

'You'll like him – he's just your cup of tea,' said Mrs
Hutchings when she told me they'd bought Barbary.
What she meant by that I wasn't sure. Mio, to me,
was my cup of tea – the horse I would have owned
had it been possible. A three-quarter Arab, beautiful, fast, with the gracefully swaying hindquarters
of the pedigree. Hindquarters which he'd used on
countless occasions to cart me off, gathering them
beneath him for his famous leap and we'd be away
up the track as if he were Pegasus.

I'd improved mind you. He didn't get away quite
so often and when he did I didn't, these days, grab the
saddle. ('Pulling leather' they call it on the Western
range, where it is regarded as the hallmark of the
dude.) No. These days I sat there, hands down, and
battled every inch of the way. We went sideways, in
circles, up on his hind legs . . . it surprised me
sometimes to realize I was doing it. 'Splendid,' Mrs
Hutchings would call. 'Now let him out gently . . .
make him trot before you canter.' I hadn't got that
part of it yet. The moment I let Mio out he went like
an arrow with a jet engine attached. But at least I
sat the arrow now with a modicum of direction: not

with my eyes shut, holding the saddle and praying.

Why then did Mrs Hutchings think I'd like Barbary?
He was another one in Mio's class, she said. Fast, eager
. . . easy to control so long as one sat him properly. And
it would be good for me to occasionally ride another
horse, particularly as we were going out to Canada
where I'd probably ride a variety anyway.

I tried Barbary. I didn't think he was like Mio. His
trot was jerkier. He didn't leap into a canter. He was
fast, admittedly, but he didn't fight control or throw
his head about, or gallop with it turned sideways, as
Mio did. Mio was better practice for prancing about
on the range – besides which, he and I had rapport.
If our land at the cottage had been flat enough and
if the Hutchings would have parted with him . . . in
spite of what I'd said about never owning horses, Mio
would have been living with us.

So I went back to riding Mio and Tina tried out
Barbary, and said she didn't like him as much as
Nutty either. His trot wasn't so smooth, she said
. . . admittedly he cantered well . . . but there
wasn't that sense of *competition*.

I knew what she meant. Tina had recently achieved
a spectacular in which, holding open the gate to the
Downs while the rest of the party went through, she'd
asked the last rider to wait, not to canter until she
herself had come through – and the other rider,
taking no notice, had gone belting after the others.
Tina, on the wrong side of the wall, had gone up
in the air on the excited Nutty and had come down

back to front. Thinking she'd then got him under control she'd turned him towards the gate – and up he'd gone again, all four feet in the air, and whirled a complete circle in the opposite direction.

Tina had fallen off, Nutty had bolted through the gate and they'd had quite a job to catch him. It was because he thought he was being left behind, of course. There was nothing vicious about Nutty. But, said Tina, she *shouldn't* have come off. So now she was insisting on opening all the gates, deliberately going through last and making him wait till she was ready. He still whipped round at every gate like a spinning top, but he'd never again managed to unseat her.

That, and trying to hold him when he raced with Mio, was what Tina regarded as competition. Not going along on Barbary, fast though he was, as uneventfully as if he were on tramlines.

For a while that was, and then Barbary began to get his bearings. He hadn't been unfit when he came – it was just that for a while before he was sold he hadn't been used much. Now his muscles were hard and he'd sized up the other horses . . . he could lick any of that lot, he said. He proceeded to do it every time they took him out, and the excursions became progressively devastating. First it was on the other rides that we heard he'd run away with someone . . . or stampeded the entire outfit, charging past it from the rear. Then it was on our ride that we would hear a warning yell from Tina and pull over to one side as Barbary came flashing through. He was getting stronger, said Tina . . . it was practically impossible to hold him. Nonsense, said Mrs Hutchings. Tina didn't sit down hard enough.

I didn't either, of course. That was a well-known fact. So it was hardly surprising, the one time in that period when I did ride Barbary, that I met with little success. Mio and Nutty were on holiday – all the horses had a fortnight's rest in turn in the summer and the two of them were out at grass together. Tina was away too, on holiday in North Africa, from which she returned quite overcome at having cantered on a camel.

Normally people only trotted on them, it seemed, held on a leading rein by an accompanying camel boy, but she'd explained that she rode in England and asked if they could go fast . . . and at the exact time that she was careering over the desert on a camel keeping up the reputation of the British for being mad, I, on her darned Barbary, was in danger of breaking my neck.

As was always my downfall, it was on a downward slope. For most of the ride I'd ridden ahead of the group, like Napoleon on his charger. Mrs Hutchings said she'd found it the safest way with people who were likely not to be able to hold him. If he took off when he was in front he wouldn't stampede the rest – in fact when he *was* in front he usually didn't bother to go. It was just his desire to show he could beat them that sent him zipping past the others.

She was right. Out in front . . . very much out in front: I had no desire to play a harp . . . I walked him, trotted, cantered, and wondered what the fuss was about. He certainly was stronger than when I'd first ridden him; even walking one could sense his sprung-steel gait. But even at his fastest he still reacted straight to the bit: I didn't have to fight to stop him, as with Mio.

Until, that was, we were on the homeward run, with the horseshoe bend ahead of us, and Mrs Hutchings, knowing my record on downward slopes, said I'd better take him, now, to the back. If I kept him well into the other horses' tails he couldn't get through if he tried. They'd be walking down it anyway, so there wouldn't be any incentive, and once we were down and round the bend . . . Well, if he took off then, I knew I could always sit him.

Unfortunately he took off before that. There we were going downhill to the bend, the horses bunched tightly, me at the back. There, on the right of the track, was an open, boulder-strewn plateau simply asking to be run away on. 'Quick! Across here!' snorted Barbary, who'd apparently been watching cowboy films on television. And across there, like escapees from an Indian war-party, we suddenly wheeled and went. Jumping rocks, narrowly missing holes, racing to cut off the others . . . who by this time, having been set off by Barbary's antics, were going like a posse themselves: sticking to the track, though, with Mrs Hutchings at their head.

'Sit down,' she shrieked across at me, but I couldn't. Not going downhill with Barbary's bouncing gait. I clung, sweating, to his neck. I saw the track reappear beneath his feet. At least we'd missed all the boulders. 'Mind the *edge*,' yelled Mrs Hutchings – and boy, now there was another snag. We'd shot across the track and now we were zooming round the horseshoe on its inside, right on the edge of the dropover.

There was nothing I could do about it. By this time Barbary had bounced my feet out of the stirrups and I could only cling to his neck and hold on. We made it, though, and once round the bend I got my stirrups back and heaved myself upright in the saddle. We went up the track as if the Apaches were after us . . . but at the end of it we stopped as suddenly as we'd started and waited placidly for the others.

'So endeth that lesson,' said Mrs Hutchings when she came up. 'It's all because you won't sit *down.*' Which wasn't what she said when, shortly afterwards, she too began to have trouble with Barbary.

Whether it was his natural behaviour, coming out now that he was on form. Whether it was that, encouraged by his success with the rest of us, he was determined to complete his record in full. Whether it was that Mrs Hutchings, seeing what he did with us, became temporarily demoralized herself . . . the fact remained that the time came when she couldn't hold him either and the rider who came belting past from the rear, shouting 'Quick! Out of the way! I'm coming!' was as likely to be her as one of us.

It created an interesting situation. As she said, she wasn't scared of him: she knew she wouldn't come off. But she couldn't very well ride him when she was shepherding children or beginners: it set a bad example to say the least. At the same time she had to try to master him – in competition with the other horses, because it was only under those conditions that he bolted . . . so when did she do her practice? When Tina and I were with her.

Nowadays there were four of us who usually rode together. Tina, myself, a girl called Penny and her husband Keith. Keith, a good rider, always had Kestrel. Penny, more nervous, generally had Kelly. With us, said Mrs Hutchings, she didn't mind. There were enough of us to block her way if she wanted to try staying at the back. We were competent enough not to chase her if Barbary was out in front. 'Oh yes, you are,' she said, seeing my eyes roll heavenwards. 'You can hold Mio if you try.'

So now we embarked on a series of rides when, instead of Mrs Hutchings shepherding us and giving us encouragement, we solicitously took care of her. 'Wait here, I'm going to try to walk him,' she would say when we got to a stretch where the horses usually cantered, and there we would sit in careful order. Mio and Kestrel in front so that, being fastest, when we did go they wouldn't tangle with the others; Nutty next so that if he did his pirouette and take-off there were two of us ahead to block him (not that Tina minded it by now but we had Mrs H. to think of); Kelly at the rear because, apart from being slowest, he kicked out if any other horse tried to pass him.

And Mrs Hutchings would advance alone, like a knight going out to joust. One step . . . two . . . Barbary would start his prancing. 'You're doing fine! You've got him!' we would call encouragingly from behind. And then she'd ease the reins the fraction necessary to allow him to go forward . . . and there'd be a sudden volcanic eruption and Barbary would be gone.

I got my practice for the prairies, all right. I got it in those vital moments after Barbary took off. When Kestrel, Mio and Nutty wanted to go too and we, to give Mrs Hutchings a breathing space, doggedly fought to hold them.

Kestrel's method of protest was to buck – and never outside of a rodeo have I seen a horse that could buck so high and wide. Keith, hat over his eyes, flew up and down on him. I, on Mio, pranced sideways, backwards and in circles. Nutty, with Tina aboard, cavorted and sidestepped behind us. Once, trying to free himself from the bit, Mio backed into Kestrel as he was bucking. Like a stone from a catapult Mio shot forward, bucking furiously too. 'For goodness sake get going!' shrieked Tina from behind us. 'I can't hold Nutty another second with you two doing that circus act!'

How right she was. The next instant she went past us like Annie Oakley, disappearing up the track in a cloud of dust. Kestrel came down from his buck and took off after Nutty. Kelly, his Irish gloom forgotten

for once, came galumphing up from the rear. So
far I'd managed to hold Mio – only because I had
him back to front, mind you, facing away from the
way he wanted to go – but now, with a wrench of
his head, he was on his hind legs . . . he'd turned,
he'd done his leap, and we were zooming after the
others. 'Like Roy Rogers,' I remember thinking as
we spun round in the air, and if only we'd had a
cine film of the incident . . .

A cameraman would have had a field day over our
escapades with Barbary. One fast horse perpetually
taking off along a track and, a few seconds later,
three equally fast ones racing after him. Sometimes,
when we caught up with her, Mrs Hutchings would
be at the end of the track, with Barbary under control
and peacefully grazing: we slowed to a trot before we
got there then, not to set him off by charging up
to him. Sometimes we misjudged and caught her
up halfway and then we all swept along together
. . . Kestrel bucking in protest because for Mrs H.'s
sake Keith wouldn't let him pass Barbary, Mio right
on Kestrel's heels, jumping sideways in mid-gallop
to avoid the bucks . . . then, finding he was on
the grass verge and that the way was clear ahead,
deciding now was the time to show the pair of them.
'Come on! Let's go!' he would snort, sticking his
head out. And I'd be practically flat on my back in
the saddle trying to stop him.

Once we lost Mrs Hutchings in a hill fog. That
was actually rather frightening. I can see her now

taking off up the track, the mist closing in behind her, and hear the staccato sound of Barbary's hooves fading gradually away in the distance. We waited longer than usual before going after her, so that we wouldn't come on her unawares in the mist and run the risk of collision. For once we were holding the horses without any trouble: they were standing there quietly grazing. Probably the fog had muffled Barbary's hoofbeats even for them, though they hadn't forgotten he was somewhere up in front. The moment we decided to go and touched our heels to their sides, they were away up the track like greyhounds.

We let them go flat out, knowing that Barbary was well ahead. We expected to find him waiting where the track we were on joined another one. We slowed as we approached the spot – but Barbary wasn't there. Probably Mrs Hutchings couldn't stop him and had gone on to the next one, we thought. So we gathered speed again and swept on. Only Barbary wasn't at the next crossing either and the track led on from there straight for the moors. The gate was a quarter of a mile ahead of us, but she wouldn't have gone out through that . . .

'Not unless he took her over it,' said someone, and we sat there imagining the worst. Barbary damaging himself out on the moors. Mrs Hutchings lying unconscious, our unable to find her because of the mist . . . which was so thick now we could hardly see each other, let alone somebody lying on the ground.

'I'm going back,' said Tina. 'I bet she never went beyond that first crossing.' 'I'll go on up to the gate,' said Keith. 'She might be waiting up there.'

Off they cantered. Penny and I stayed where we were and shouted. Our voices echoed back as if to mock us. Tina returned. 'No sign of her,' she said. So we sat in the silent fog and waited for Keith . . . and he didn't come back either.

Eventually the three of us set off towards the gate, wondering what he might have found . . . or whether he'd met up with misfortune, too, and in turn hadn't been able to stop Kestrel. We intended to trot. We couldn't see a thing in the fog and any moment Kestrel might be coming back towards us. But Mio wasn't going to be left out of all this dashing about: this was one of the times when I was still unable to hold him.

Off up the track he roared, Nutty and Kelly in pursuit, and sure enough suddenly, out of the fog, came Kestrel. We reined like troopers: we were getting pretty good at it: we certainly got enough practice. 'She isn't up at the gate,' reported Keith. 'I've been looking round for tracks, but there's just no sign of her anywhere.'

We started back for the stables. Obviously there'd have to be a search party and the sooner it got started the better. Lynn Hutchings, for instance, knew every inch of the moors, and as an expert rider would cover it faster than any of us. We'd have to call the police, too. Probably they'd bring in tracker dogs. Where was the nearest point to the road, to get a stretcher? We looked at the various sidetracks as we rode back the way we'd come, but decided against trying any of them. There were so many. We could so easily miss her in the fog. Better to get straight back and get an organized search started.

Which was how we came to meet up with her. Sitting patiently on Barbary, in the fog, at the crossing where we'd first expected to see her. She'd waited for us, she said – Barbary had been perfectly under control – then she'd heard us thundering up the track, so she'd taken him up a side-path so he wouldn't be set off again by our coming. And there she'd sat like a Sioux scout while the four of us shot past . . . hidden from us by a swirl of mist, no doubt: certainly we hadn't seen her. She'd gone on then, intending to take a short cut and catch us up, which must have been how Tina missed her . . . but the fog had thickened so she had turned back, reckoning that we would, too, when we couldn't find her.

We rode back silently for a while, limp with relief, then I began to laugh. 'What's so funny?' asked Tina. 'Only that Mrs Hutchings is supposed to be looking after *us*,' I said. 'You'd think we were teaching *her*!'

Chapter Four

Nothing ever happens in our village without somebody being around to see it. Fred Ferry, for instance,
had been in the forest that day in the mist. Don't ask
me why, except that he always seems to be up there,
just as Father Adams appears to live perpetually in
ambush over our garden wall.

'He says,' said Father Adams, coming in to tell us
what Fred had been broadcasting up in the Rose and
Crown . . . 'he says thee wust careerin' about up there
like a buzz-fly under a meat-cover 'n he wondered
whatever was goin' on. 'N then he seed thic bloke
come tearin' out of the fog and the rest of thee stop
dead with thee in front, and he realized what tothers
was doin' was tryin' to stiffen thee nerve.'

It was no use trying to put him right. There is an
amazing echo in this valley. Often I've stood in the
cottage garden and heard the sound of horses galloping up on one of the forest tracks. So clearly that
I could tell how many there were, where they started
cantering and when they stopped again, and hear the
riders' voices calling to each other. In the same way,
so many people had heard our carryings-on during
the time of the trials with Barbary . . . the sounds

of frenzied galloping, the yells to 'Look out!' and 'For heaven's sake *hold* him!' . . . that they had no difficulty in believing Fred Ferry's version and the story went round like wildfire.

'You've got yourselves insured for this trip, have you?' asked one of our neighbours – looking at me, I noticed, not at Charles – while Miss Wellington, when it got to her ears, came scurrying down immediately; the first time we'd seen her in weeks.

She was so worried, she said. If only she'd spared more time for us she might have persuaded us not to be so rash as to think of going. As we knew, though, she'd had other things on her mind . . . though thank goodness that was all settled now.

We were glad to hear it. When Miss Wellington gets intense about something the oddest situations are likely to ensue. One result of the arrival of the Bannetts, for instance, had been that when the Rector went to call on her one day he couldn't find anywhere to put his hat. All eight pegs of Miss Wellington's hallstand, usually chastely garnished with her gardening hat, her shopping hat and her sou-wester, were festooned with men's headgear. Trilbies cloth caps, a dented bowler . . . the Rector was quite startled, wondering what had happened until out bustled Miss Wellington, whipping off the hats like a pile of pancakes, exhorting him to please hang his up *anywhere,* these were only there to scare off strangers.

Including, obviously, the Bannetts. It seemed that Miss Wellington had a cousin in town who always kept

a man's hat on her hallstand to ward off intruders
and Miss Wellington, inspired by this and carrying it
as usual to excess, had decided that eight hats would
be even better. She'd bought them at a jumble sale
and the effect was quite spectacular. Understandable
when she explained it, as she did to the Rector, but
pretty rivetting when spotted by the milkman, or by
people peering in as they passed.

Some interesting theories had gone round about
those hats, particularly since Miss Wellington, to add
authenticity to their being there, had taken to opening her back door and shouting 'Frank' into the
garden at odd intervals . . . followed, according to
some observers, by her creeping along the hedge
between her cottage and the Bannetts' at dusk with
one of the hats bobbing above it on a stick. Fred Ferry,
of course, insisted he'd seen a *real* bloke. 'Different
'un every night,' he elaborated, capitalizing on the
fact of the several hats, and though nobody believed
him for a moment it was just as well, rumour adding
to itself as it does, that Miss Wellington had come to
the end of that particular little fantasy. Or at least,
we hoped she had.

What had led her to the discovery that the Bannetts
were, as she put it, 'like us,' was her worrying, after
several weeks had passed, because she hadn't con-
formed to village etiquette and called on them. Few
people had. For one thing both of them worked
and were away all day; for another, people don't
do this calling business quite so much these days;

for a third they were undoubtedly a *bit* odd . . .
So far as we were concerned this would have been
a reason *for* calling, having the reputation of being
odd ourselves, except that we'd been so busy getting ready to go to Canada . . . Anyway, having
worried herself into her usual state of expecting
to be punished by the Almighty at any moment if
she didn't forthwith do whatever it was she had left
undone, Miss Wellington had tapped timidly on the
Bannetts' door one evening bearing a bottle of her
elderflower wine. Liz had asked her in, and when
she saw six tortoises basking in a semi-circle in the
Bannetts' fireplace, her doubts, she told us earnestly,
had been stilled immediately.

Most people's doubts would more likely have
increased, particularly since each of the tortoises
was tucked up separately in a bedroom slipper.
Not Miss Wellington's however. 'That dear boy has
loved tortoises since he was a child,' she informed us
rapturously. 'There was one at his infant school, in
the sandpit, that wasn't being cared for properly, and
he insisted, even then, on taking it home and looking
after it himself. And that dear girl puts them into slippers to keep them off the flagstone floor. They bring
them in from their pen at night because a couple of
them have colds . . . and those two dear things light
a fire every evening to keep the tortoises warm.'

Also, to keep the record straight, because they were
thrilled with their open fireplace and liked to see a
log fire burning in it. It was a long time yet to winter

and the tortoises provided a good excuse – though there was no doubt either that they liked the heat. We saw them ourselves in due course. Six slippers fanned out in front of the fire, a small tortoise already asleep in two of them – and four big ones doggedly trying to clamber over each other on to the hearthstone, heads outstretched to what must have seemed to them like the warmth of the Caribbean, while Liz prepared hot milk for the pair that had the colds.

Add to that the fact that the Bannetts not only liked her elderflower wine but had embarked on making it themselves . . . their inglenook, where it wasn't occupied by tortoises, was now packed with glugging gallon jars plus a couple of carboys for good measure . . . and Miss Wellington was well away. Tim with that beard, she told us, looked exactly like the photograph of her father as a young man that hung over the tallboy in her bedroom . . . and had I noticed that the long red string of Florentine beads that Liz wore was just like the one she had herself, only hers was blue? I had. As I'd noticed that there wasn't much difference in the vaguely flowing dresses the pair of them wore, either, except that Miss Wellington's were the real vintage twenties and Liz's were mod-shop copies. Pass for mother and daughter they would . . . or rather for niece and slightly dotty great-aunt. Miss Wellington's ship had really come home. She had a pair of young fledglings to fuss over.

So had we. Four of them to be exact. Still happily occupying our garage with their parents and, with a fortnight to go to our departure date, showing no sign whatever of vacating it. The garage door still leant against the plum-tree with Father Adams and his cronies passing comment on it – though to be honest, by this time we were beset by so many other pitfalls that a garage without a door was the least among our worries.

Shebalu had started the ball rolling, four weeks before we were due to go, by being sick and refusing to eat. This was a phenomenon in itself. At two years old she'd never been known to miss a meal in her life and usually had to be shut in the hall while Seeley, who was a slow eater, finished, or she'd have polished off his as well. After a day of watching her languish round the place like Camille . . . sitting in the middle of the floor looking fragile; turning her head wanly when we offered her food; answering us, when we spoke to her, in a faint little voice that indicated she was going any moment now but she forgave us for being Unkind to her . . . we called the Vet. We couldn't take a chance, we told him. If she was incubating anything we must know at once. Not only would we not go away if she were ill but, even if she meanwhile fully recovered, she certainly couldn't go to Low Knap because of the danger to other cats.

Not to worry, he said after he'd examined her. His bet, bearing in mind the hot weather, was that she'd either been catching flies and eating them, or food on which a fly had pitched. He'd give her an injection by way of precaution, but he was sure it was just a passing stomach upset. If it was catching, Seeley would give us an indication fast enough, he added encouragingly. He'd go down with it too, probably within a week.

That, then, took care of the fourth week from departure date. Watching over Shebalu, feeling like jumping for joy when she at last sniffed faintly at my finger dipped in salmon paste . . . sniffed it again and then began to lick with fervour . . . and then concentrating our vigil on Seeley. It still *could* have been an infection which Shebalu had taken only lightly. Any moment now Seeley, too, could go off his food.

He didn't. No more, anyway, than was occasioned by his indignation when he found me hanging around watching him every time he attempted to eat. Why was I doing That? he kept on wailing at me aggrievedly. Didn't I know it put him Off? Couldn't he even enjoy his minced pig's heart in Private?

By which time we'd arrived at three weeks prior to departure date and Charles's Aunt Ethel announced that she was dying. This in itself was not unusual. Any time for the past twenty years any of the family had gone on holiday, she always decided she was dying. Not usually on the telephone at half-past eight in the morning, though, sounding as though she was fading fast and asking weakly for Charles.

Panic-stricken I fetched him, hovering anxiously while he spoke to her. 'Put your teeth in, Aunt,' he said almost at once. (So that was the reason

for the feeble old-lady voice.) 'No, you're *not* talking to an angel. Put your hearing aid in. No you
haven't, otherwise I'd hear it oscillating. Put it in
now. IMMEDIATELY.'

All was well, as was confirmed when, more or
less normal communication having been achieved,
Charles said he'd ring her doctor and she quavered
that it was too late now for that. The slightest thing
really wrong with her and it was the doctor who rang
us, Aunt Edith having summoned him personally, not
risking any delay by dealing through intermediaries.
Charles checked with the doctor nevertheless – who
said that she was likely to reach a hundred but he,
Dr Cartwright, wasn't: not with Aunt Edith ringing
him at six in the morning twice already that week
to ask should she have All Bran for breakfast. And
on we went to week two from departure date, when
things really began to happen.

We'd been trying for months to arrange for the
hire, in Canada, of a single-unit camper – the sort
which carries its own water supply and refrigerator
and has a made-up bed over the driving cabin. So
far every firm we'd contacted was either fully booked
for the season or its campers were king-size, luxury-
type, and correspondingly expensive. Now, suddenly,
up came CP Air with the offer of a small Mazda
four-berth camper, based on Edmonton to which
our flights were booked, and – it seemed like a
miracle at this point of the summer – available from
mid-July through to September.

The manager of CP Air's London office rang up and we clinched the deal on the spot – which achievement Charles, relieved to know that he wasn't after all going to have to sleep out on the prairie wrapped in a blanket, celebrated by going out and putting in his runner-bean sticks. Ten- and twelve-foot-high hazel branches which reared skywards like teepee poles and when Ern Biggs enquired why he hadn't trimmed them off at the normal six feet – 'To encourage the beans,' Charles lightheartedly informed him. 'It'll give them something to aim for.' Ern looked at the youthful bean plants, up at the heights to which they were supposed to aspire, back again at Charles with his mouth open and headed speedily down the lane to Father Adams.

'They'll have to pick the ruddy things with a ladder,' his disbelieving voice came floating up to us while Charles, already mentally at the wheel of our camper, bean-poled blissfully on.

So blissful was he that when, next day, there was a telephone call from Canada House passing on an invitation for us to be guests of the City of Edmonton for their Klondike Days festivities . . . and please could we let them have our measurements so that our costumes could be ready for us on arrival . . . Charles voted immediate acceptance of that as well.

We could hardly have turned it down seeing that the Canadian Government was sponsoring our trip but it gave me an uneasy moment or two when I considered the implications. Victorian costumes,

they'd said. Charles for five whole *days* in a Victorian
topper and tailcoat when he practically had to be
straitjacketed to get him into tails for a three-hour
wedding? Probably with a frill-fronted shirt and string
tie as well, and carrying a gold-topped cane into the
bargain?

Leaving, like Scarlett O'Hara, the possibilities of
that situation to take care of themselves, I concurred
in accepting the invitation and we swept on to one
week from departure date – when Aunt Edith rang
us four times in one evening with the information
that she was definitely weakening and if she didn't
see us again she hoped we'd enjoy ourselves; with a
last-minute flash of inspiration, as the swallows still
showed no sign of moving out, we re-hung the garage
door but removed the glass from a window high in the
apex, so they could use that way in and out instead;
Shebalu jumped out of our bedroom window, which
I'd forgotten to close, at five o'clock one morning
(that was all right too, though; she must have landed
on the lawn and when I panicked downstairs to look
for the body she appeared unconcernedly through
the back gate, nattering happily about what a Fine
Day it was and why weren't the rest of us up yet); and
Charles, small wonder after all we'd been through,
developed a tooth infection.

We made it though. On the allotted day, against
all odds, we finally flew out to Edmonton: Charles
with a supply of penicillin tablets which he had to
take every four hours; me a bag of nerves in case his

infection got worse in mid-Atlantic. And suddenly we could see Hudson Bay below us, and there we were. Coming down over the North-West Territories . . . the Athabasca River and the barren lands north of Edmonton, covered with muskeg and dotted, as far as the eye could see, with hundreds of little lakes that looked, from the air, like puddles . . . And finally Edmonton itself, its tall buildings golden in the late afternoon sunlight, and beyond it the Canadian prairie, rolling away to the south.

Chapter Five

We could hardly believe it. We remembered Edmonton from two years previously as an outstandingly modern city. The Oil Capital of Canada, with more than 7,000 producing oil wells within a hundred-mile radius. A city of wide streets, beautiful buildings, a magnificent University complex perched high above the North Saskatchewan River and an energetically youthful population – 72% of them under 40 years of age, according to statistics – whose brisk-looking, brief-cased businessmen travelled by air-bus to Calgary or Vancouver as matter-of-factly as Brighton residents catch a train to London.

Now, driving into it in the airport limousine, we seemed to have gone eighty years back in time. A stagecoach passed us, creaking on its springs, a guard with a shotgun sitting beside the driver. Women swept along the pavements in bustles and flower-piled hats as though they had never in their lives worn anything else. The streets themselves looked odd . . . suddenly we realized what it was. The buildings had false painted fronts. Wooden-fronted saloons, a barber's shop with red-and-white striped pole, an old-time jail . . . the Hertz rent-a-car offices disguised as stables, offering mules for hire. Tied up at the Bank of Montreal's entrance, where a sign said 'Deposit Your Gold Here,' there actually was a mule, complete with prospector's kit of pick, shovel, gold-panning sieve and bedroll.

Another mule was tethered outside the Château Lacombe hotel where we were to stay – where the traffic was held up, to let the bus turn into the courtyard, by a frock-tailed Victorian policeman with a truncheon at his belt and where, standing in the hotel lobby while Charles registered us in, I felt like the principal character in one of those Bateman cartoons. Me in scarlet trouser suit and big sling air-bag and every other person in the lobby straight out of frontier history.

Even the group of businessmen emerging from one of the hotel conference rooms were in the appropriate gear. Magenta, dove-grey and powder-blue tailcoats, peg-top trousers and elastic-sided boots. Not one of them looked in the least self-conscious, either, as one would expect men to be in such clothes – because, it seems, they do this every year and would look more incongruous if they didn't.

It is Edmonton's way of remembering the famous Gold Rush of 1898, when the city, then little more than a Hudson's Bay fur-trading post halfway to the frozen north, became important overnight as one of the bases for miners heading for the Klondike. As a realistic way of commemorating history – not by speeches and exhibitions but by a halcyon,

rip-roaring fortnight in July when Edmonton goes
into costume en masse . . . when roulette wheels
turn in saloons again, waiters in striped aprons
scuttle around carrying clutches of beer mugs,
go into a bank and you'll be served, without his
turning a hair, by a cashier wearing straw boater,
butcher-striped waistcoat and sleeve-garters – there
can be few experiences to equal it.

Our own costumes were waiting for us in our
room and I, one of my lifelong dreams being
to have lived in the gay Nineties, was into mine
like a shot. So was Charles, without a word of
protest . . . in fact he appeared to be rather
pleased with himself. We surveyed each other. He
in an olive-green tailcoat, green-striped trousers,
kingfisher-blue brocade waistcoat, buff top-hat and
gold-topped cane, I in a pink slipper-satin Mae
West dress with a huge cartwheel hat trimmed
with ostrich feathers. 'Whoever would have thought
a trip to see Canadian wildlife would start like this,'
said Charles. 'What on earth would the village
think if they could see us now?'

What indeed. Particularly in the days that followed,
when Charles, entering thoroughly into his Victorian
dandy role, sang a microphone duet at a public
luncheon with Klondike Kate, and he and I, together
with David Hunn, then Sports Correspondent of *The
Observer*, danced Knees Up Mother Brown, by request
of the audience, on the stage of the Silver Slipper
Saloon. As Britishers – the only ones in the party of

writers and photographers – apparently we added
authenticity to the occasion. I lost my shoes, Charles
practically dislocated himself, but we did the British
pioneers of the 1890s proud!

The whole thing was like a dream. One morning we had breakfast with the Mounties. Not the
khaki-shirted R.C.M.P. of modern times with their
peaked caps and streamlined police cars, but men
in the scarlet tunics, blue riding breeches and wide-
brimmed hats that represented law on the prairies in
the old days. It reminded me irrepressibly of a scene
from *Rose Marie* – with due apologies to the Mounties
themselves, who wince at the name of Nelson Eddy!

Sitting at a huge round table, eating bacon and
eggs and muffins and honey, we talked of horses
and riding and of being out on the trail. Even so,
when I kicked what I thought was some dropped
cutlery and bent to pick it up, and realized that
in fact it was the jingling of my neighbour's spurs
. . . sturdy silver spurs with chains on them, fastened
to the traditional black R.C.M.P. riding boots . . .
it brought home to me with a surge of joy that I
was back in my beloved West. Even in the cities
the outdoors is not very distant.

Certainly not in Edmonton, where from the window of our hotel room we could look out, beyond
the tall white buildings and wide, straight-running
streets, to where the prairie waited for us. A mist
of burnt-yellow and blue in the distance, stretching on as far as the eye could see. Five days to

go before we set out on our own trail. Meanwhile we enjoyed our Klondike Days.

We did enjoy them, too. Normally we live quiet country lives. Sophistication is not our cup of tea. But this sophistication . . . the nightclubs, the receptions, the huge luncheon given by the Toronto and Dominion Bank . . . all of it was overlaid with a country-style flavour that was irresistible, like a gigantic Harvest Home that just went on and on. Country-style, yet tempered with old-time elegance. Wearing those costumes seemed to have an effect on people. Women moved with grace, men became much courtlier . . . opening doors, doffing their toppers with a flourish, bowing the ladies through. Which is how Charles, who is always courtly, made history at the Château Lacombe.

Charles always ushers ladies through turnstiles and doorways ahead of him. The number of times I've gone through a theatre foyer or a Customs barrier with Charles as I think, right behind me . . . and when the official holds out his hand and I turn to indicate my husband, who has the tickets or our joint passport, as the case may be, there he is, with about eight females between me and him, politely waving them on . . .

It was a foregone conclusion, therefore, that Charles in 1890s' costume would be courtlier than ever. Always last out of the hotel lift, for instance, having ushered everybody out ahead of him – though normally it didn't matter in the least. Usually our party filled the whole of the lift and we all got out at the same floor.

On this occasion, however, we had an additional couple on board. In Klondike costume, of course, so nobody really noticed. And at our appointed floor our party trooped out, dispersing towards its various rooms. We had ten minutes flat in which to freshen up and meet again, ready for the next sortie, down in the hotel lobby.

The rest of the party dispersed, that is. As I stood there waiting for Charles to come out of the lift he politely gestured the remaining pair to precede him, the woman stepped forward in her aquamarine bustle . . . pressed the lift button with the point of her parasol and, right before my very eyes, the lift doors closed and off soared Charles.

Apparently, the next thing was that Charles explained he'd wanted to get out there, and the woman tried to halt the lift by running her finger down all the buttons from top to bottom before he or her husband could stop her. This produced the galvanizing effect (the couple themselves getting out two floors up) that the lift, with Charles as its solitary occupant, went on stopping at every floor, right on up to the twenty-fourth with the revolving restaurant on the top, and then began to descend again, opening and closing at every stop.

On the way up the doors had parted to reveal a man in a maroon frock-coat standing on one of the landings, waiting for a downward lift. He didn't half look surprised, said Charles, when the doors opened on the downward descent and there was Charles, still in solitary glory, now on his way down. Even more surprised when, he having pressed the button for the lobby, the lift continued to stop and open automatically at every floor going down. Nobody was waiting to get in, of course; it was the result of the woman pressing all the buttons.

Unfortunately Charles got so engrossed in explaining this that when the lift eventually arrived back at the twelfth floor Charles didn't realize it and so didn't get out. I wasn't on the landing to signal to him, being busy, by that time, trying to find a maid with a key to our room . . . our ten minutes' breather was nearly up and we were due down in the lobby almost at once. And so it was that when Charles, having descended floor by floor to the lobby where a fascinated audience had gathered to watch the phenomenal progress of the lift flashes, smiled at them disarmingly and started back up again . . . when he eventually arrived once more at the twelfth floor and the door opened upon the landing, the rest of our party was gathered there, waiting now to go down.

Unruffled, courteous as ever, Charles stood aside to let them get in. 'Oh no you don't!' I said, grabbing him before he could do it again.

It was that afternoon, following lunch at the Old Spaghetti Factory which we made, thanks to the lift descent, by the skin of our teeth, that we met our first-ever grizzly. Not in the remoteness of the Rockies, as we'd expected, but in a Game Park fifteen miles from Edmonton. And if that sounds tame . . . it isn't if you do as I did, and feed a full-grown grizzly with a feeding bottle. One of the biggest grizzlies in captivity, weighing six times as much as a man.

It was the idea of the Edmonton Travel Manager, with whom we'd been talking over our plans. There were wolves in Jasper National Park, he told us – though we'd be lucky if we saw them in the summer. There were grizzlies in the mountains around Waterton . . . we knew that for ourselves, of course. We'd heard stories about them on our previous visit. It was one of the reasons we were going back to Waterton. But, said the Travel Manager, if we went out to the Alberta Game Farm we could talk with experts on the subject. They could tell us a lot about them. They actually had three full-grown grizzlies, and Canadian lynx and cougar, and deer and prairie buffalo.

They did, and the sight of the animals in their natural surroundings is one we shall long remember. I don't like zoos, but the Game Farm is something different, with such large enclosures that in many of them you can't see the boundaries. Some of the animals there would be extinct by now but for dedicated projects like this, striving for their protection. Particularly we were impressed by the colony of timber wolves, safe there from poisoning or shooting, wandering, reticent from people as is of homoeopathy to a tome, heavy with thick paper, woodcuts and small print, which seemed – it was in German Gothic – to be a treatise on botany. I found translations of Dioscorides and Galen, reprints of the herbals of Culpeper and Gerard and John Parkinson, at least half a dozen books on the planning and planting of herb gardens, and several on wild plants and their uses, side by side with exotics like *Maori Medicines*, and *A Witch-doctor Remembers*.

And that was the crop. There were recipes in plenty, ranging from simple things like mint and comfrey tea to 'wrap the kumaras in puriri leaves and bake slowly over hot stones, then dry in the sun for two weeks', but no sign at all of Goody Gostelow. The only real find of the afternoon was on the top shelf, when I lifted out three volumes of somebody's treatise on the edible and poisonous fungi of Europe.

Behind the books, dusty but still gleaming, was the crystal globe that Cousin Geillis and I had looked into on that day by the River Eden.

I stopped at four o'clock for a cup of tea and a visit to the toolshed, then got back to work. By the time I had finished, and the books were all back in place, it was growing dark, and my back and arms were aching. I had a bath, then fed the dog, and made supper for Hodge and myself in the kitchen. Afterwards, for the first time, I set a match to the drawing-room fire, and soon had a cheerful bright blaze, with the light dwelling on the pretty cretonnes and polished furniture and the glass of the bookcase.

18

I made myself some lunch, fed Hodge and the dog, and spent some time with the latter. He was more relaxed now, seemed pleased to see me, and managed to wag fully half his tail as he ate a mixture of brown bread and chicken scraps softened with chicken stock. When I let him out for a few minutes he showed no desire to run away, but did his business and then retreated into the safety of the shed. I locked the door on him again and went back into the house.

I had promised to look for the 'special' recipe book, and if I could find it and hand it over to Agnes, it might keep the Trapps away, at least until I could get the dog temporarily out of the way. I suspected that what Agnes really wanted was not a recipe for something like bramble jelly – what could be special about that? – but the secrets of some of Cousin Geillis's cures. As far as I was concerned, she could have them. One thing I was certain about, they would do no harm to anyone.

I had locked the inventory, along with the copy of

my cousin's will, in the desk in the den. I got it out, took it into the drawing-room, and sat down to read it through.

It was arranged room by room. I started by skimming quickly through the contents of the room I was in, furniture, soft goods, pictures, ornaments . . . As far as I could see without detailed checking, everything was there. Last came the contents of the big bookcase. This, if I was to be accurate, would require a detailed check, but for the moment a rapid glance down the list must suffice. When I had cleaned the room I had spent a long time over the shelves, and could more or less remember what was there. It was a rich collection; novels, one or two biographies (like me, she had little taste for them); a full collection of travel books, that is, travellers' accounts of exotic countries. Books about animals; three full shelves on birds; another on butterflies and moths, and two on trees, flowers and grasses. But the main – and most attractive – section was on gardens and garden plants. I glanced at some of the latter; the books on plants were a gardener's selection, not a herbalist's. There was nothing here that could be called a recipe book.

In any case Agnes Trapp had had access to these shelves, as to the cookery books in the kitchen and the few reference books in the den, so the still-room was really the only likely place.

I leafed through the inventory and found it, 'stillroom contents', a series of formidable lists; page after page of chemicals or distillations, all those bottles and jars named and in order. A mercifully short list of

furnishings followed, then, finally, three full pa
books.

But no trouble there; no trouble at all. The fir
was underlined in red. The only one to be so
guished. And its title made it sure.

Goody Gostelow's own Home Remedies and Re
Goody Gostelow, the old lady who had lived he
seventy years, whose reputation as a witch had p
right on to Cousin Geillis and now, after a fashi
me. Goody Gostelow, expert on magic, who had
Thornyhold into an enchanted stronghold to ke
evil and allow the good to grow and ripen.
Home Remedies for healing had presumably
studied and followed by my cousin.

Whose recipes Agnes Trapp was so very anxi
see.

I checked that the doors were locked, then
duster and went upstairs.

At first glance I could see nothing that mi
Goody Gostelow's book, but there were doz
volumes, some of them much used, some even
with handling, and it would be easy to miss a sm
tucked inside another. I set to work, methodicall
the books out in sections, examine them one by o
them, and return them to the shelves. It was hea
And it was slow, not only because I cleaned ea
before returning it to its shelf, but because t
were fascinating, and I lingered over many of
its kind, it seemed to be a comprehensive and p
valuable collection. I was no judge of its com
but there seemed to be everything, from a kind

As I went to draw the curtains Hodge, who had followed me into the room, asked to be let out of the French windows. I obliged him, then, after a moment's thought, followed him out and went round to the toolshed. This time the dog – I must try to think of him as Rags – met me just inside the door, and let me lead him round and back into the house. I sat down in one of the arm-chairs with a book I had noticed earlier, *Pigeons, How to Keep and Care for Them*, but kept my eyes on the dog. For a few minutes he wandered uneasily round the room, sniffing, exploring, with frequent glances back at me, and the tail ready to wave whenever he caught my eye.

'Rags?' I tried it, and he came, and was patted and soothed, and finally, with a sigh, he settled himself down beside my chair, nose on paws, blinking at the flames.

It was a long, peaceful evening. The dog slept, only rousing when I got up to put a log on the fire. I could not guess whether he was used to a house and a hearthrug, but he certainly took to mine with no hesitation. Finally came the sound I had been waiting for, Hodge's demand to be let in. I glanced at Rags. He raised his head, eyed the window and wagged his tail, but did not move. I crossed the room and opened the window. In came Hodge, stopped dead, blew himself up to a formidable size, and spat furiously. Rags lay still, wagging that ingratiating tail. The cat advanced. The dog shrank nearer to my chair, abasing himself.

Watching the duel of wills, I was satisfied. The dog obviously knew cats and liked them; the cat, the dominant animal, would take time to get used to the dog's presence, but knew himself to be in no danger. A week or two, and all would be well.

I sat for a while longer, watchful over my book, while the dog went back to a wakeful doze and Hodge stalked, with great dignity, to the arm-chair on the other side of the fire and settled, with frequent pauses to glare at the dog, to washing himself.

A movement on the table at my elbow caught my attention. The globe. I had set it down there and forgotten it, and the firelight was moving over it, light and shadow, colour and darkness.

> *Black spirits and white, red spirits and grey,*
> *Mingle, mingle, mingle, you that mingle may!*

It was bad luck to quote from *Macbeth*, wasn't it? But then that particular rhyme was not from *Macbeth* itself, but only quoted from some older witch-play . . .

Hodge, the witch's cat, with one leg still held rigidly upright, had stopped his washing and was staring at the globe. His eyes were wide and bright, but his fur lay sleek, newly licked and unruffled. He looked interested, no more.

I picked it up, held it between my hands, and stared into it myself.

They were still there, among the shadow and the flames; the flight of pigeons. It was like looking into one of those old paperweights, which, when shaken, loose a snow-storm. Flock after flock of pigeons wheeled and circled, then, while I watched, coalesced into one shimmering cloud of flight and sank slowly to rest.

★   ★   ★

Rags seemed happy to go back to his bed in the toolshed. I left him there with a biscuit and a bowl of fresh water, then set a saucer of milk in the kitchen for Hodge while I locked up. Hodge, still slightly edgy, but mollified by the dog's banishment and the soothing ritual of bedtime, stalked ahead of me up the stairs and vanished into my bedroom.

One part of the evening ritual remained. I filled the water-jug for the pigeons, and went upstairs to the attic.

I believe I had expected it, but all the same I stood there for several seconds, while the superstitious flesh crept on my arms. There were three pigeons now, on perches side by side. They shuffled and cooed. Nothing could have looked more innocent than these birds of peace, these messengers of the dead.

The new one was different yet again, blue-grey, its breast glimmering with iris. It regarded me placidly with garnet eyes as I reached out and lifted it from its perch.

There was a message on its leg. Of course there was. Gently I removed this, put the bird back, put food down and poured fresh water into the trough before I unfolded the screw of paper. The birds flew down to the grain, and the newcomer dipped its head to drink.

Standing directly under the unshaded electric bulb I unfolded the thin fragment of paper.

It was different writing. A thin printing in capitals: WELCOME TO THORNYHOLD AND GOD BLESS YOUR SLEEP, it said, No signature.

I crossed to the window, and stood for a long time

looking out at the fading colours of the sky, where, on that extraordinary night, I had seen the owls and the beckoning light, and had flown through and over those high whispering trees. I had always been content to know that there was more in the living world than we could hope to understand. Now I found myself drifting on the peace of belief. Even if it meant that that 'nightmare' had been the truth, I thought I could accept it. *God bless your sleep.* Perhaps if I forgot the other long-past nightmares, and recalled the good things of my childhood and what I had been taught, He would.

19

I guessed that Agnes would not want to wait for me to take her the coveted book, and I was right. She came up soon after breakfast. Before the back door rattled and Hodge vanished upstairs, the toolshed window had been obscured, the dog fed and admonished to silence, the globe was locked away in the desk with the inventory, and I was in the kitchen washing pots for the bramble jelly.

'Well, Miss Ramsey?' was her greeting. She had been hurrying. She was breathless and her colour was high.

I greeted her warmly. 'Oh, Agnes, I'm so glad you've come! I was going to come down later, but I quite forgot to do this jelly yesterday, and I thought I'd better get on with it. Nearly two pints of juice – that's not bad, is it? And now I wonder—'

'You said you'd look out for that book.' Sharp. Accusing.

'Yes. That's what made me forget the jelly. I found

the inventory, and I've been through all the books in the place, along with the lists. It took ages. There is one that sounds exciting, and I wondered – but for the moment, can you tell me, please, about this jelly? I can't find any special recipe, so I'm just going by the one I know. A pound of sugar to a pint of juice, and I did manage to find a few windfall apples in the orchard—'

'It'll do.' She almost snapped it. The flush had deepened, but not, I thought, at my reference to the stripped fruit trees. It was anger. But she left the matter aside for a moment to show me the gift which, as usual, she had brought me. She dumped a big basket of blackberries on the table with a rap that set the fruit jumping. 'Brought you these. I told you there was plenty near by us. And I put some of our crab-apples in, too. Do as well as anything to make a good set.'

'Well, thank you! How very kind.' I seemed to be saying that, with various shades of insincerity, almost every hour on the hour. 'That'll save me another trip to the quarry.'

'That's right.' Suddenly, from the look in her eye, quickly veiled, I knew that that was exactly why she had picked and brought the fruit. Why on earth should it be to her advantage to stop me going over there again? I shrugged it off mentally, and turned away from her, stirring the juice.

Behind me, she said, sharply: 'About the book.'

'Oh, yes. I gather you'd seen this book? I mean, you do know that my cousin had it?'

'Oh, yes.'

'Well, the first one in the still-room inventory seemed the likeliest one to me. It was called *Goody Gostelow's own Home Remedies and Receipts*.' I glanced back at her. 'Was that the title you remember?'

'That'd be it!' The blue eyes shone with excitement. 'That'd be it!'

'I thought it might,' I said, stirring. 'But I'm afraid it isn't there.'

'What do you mean, it isn't there?'

'Just what I say. There's a list in the inventory of all the books in the shelves, and as far as I can make out, all the others are there, but not that one. Maybe she lent it to someone?'

Her voice rose. 'She wouldn't do that! She couldn't! If she was going to let anybody take a look at it, that would be me. If it's gone to old Madge . . . but she wouldn't do that! Not Miss Saxon!'

I looked at her curiously. My look seemed to bring her to herself. She said, more calmly: 'The Widow Marget that lives over to Tidworth. No friend of mine. Nor no friend of Miss Saxon's neither, I shouldn't think.'

'Then she probably didn't lend her the book. But if you know her, why don't you ask her next time you go that way?'

'I might, at that,' said Agnes. She sat down at the table. Her fingers were plucking at her skirt. She looked sulky and deflated. For the first time since I had met her, I felt sorry for her, without quite knowing why.

I stirred the jelly. 'Did you ever actually see the book?'

'Once. But Miss Saxon wasn't one for letting her recipes out, and she took it away before I could get anything much puzzled out.'

'Did she never give you any of her recipes?'

'Oh, yes, the comfrey salve and some of the teas. But the rest she kept. She gave me a medicine once for mother's cough that was sovereign. That was her word, sovereign. I'd rightly like a look at that one before the winter comes.'

'Of course.' I bent to sniff at the boiling juice. It smelled done. I spooned a little out on to a cold plate. 'Agnes, you said you couldn't get it "puzzled out". Do you mean it was handwritten?'

'Oh, yes, it was in writing, and some of it very faint and scratchy. Terrible hard to read, it was. But I'm no great reader of books, anyway!'

The jelly wrinkled to a set on the plate as I tilted it. I lifted the jelly pan over to the table, and took the warm jars from above the Aga. 'I did hear something about Goody Gostelow – Lady Sibyl. Mr Dryden told me. I was thinking that, if she lived so long ago, and with all the – well, the stories about her, the book might have some sort of value. So perhaps the lawyers have it, or my cousin may have put it in the bank, or something. Don't be upset. I'll find it, and let you know.'

She looked mollified. 'Well, I'll be glad. Not that it's desperate, but when people promise something, and people have looked forward to something . . .' She let it hang. 'That jelly looks all right. Here, let me, I'll sort the covers for you. You did look on all the shelves?'

'What? Yes, I did. You know yourself that it's not

here in the kitchen, or in the drawing-room or the den. I'm sure I didn't miss it in the still-room, but you can look for yourself if you like. That's the key there on the dresser.'

My very readiness must have reassured her. She shook her head. 'Not if you've looked. I'm not so handy with books, myself. It'll turn up, maybe. If you ask at the lawyer's, I'll maybe go and see the Widow Marget. There, that's the labels done. I'll help you pick these new brambles over.'

She found a big bowl, tipped the blackberries from her basket, and sat down again at the table.

I finished pouring the jelly, and set the pots aside to cool. Four pots I got, and felt absurdly proud of myself as the sunlight, streaming through the window, made the rich colour glow more beautifully even than wine.

'Good enough for the jam tent at the show?' I asked her, laughing.

'I said you'd not got a lot to learn.' Picking busily, she darted a look at me. It was a friendly one, and smiling. 'That's done for the year, the show, I mean, but there'll be others. Some day, maybe, you'll go along o' me to meet the other ladies? We've meetings all year.'

'Well, thank you. I think I'd like to.' I laughed again. 'But not to show my home cooking. Not yet, anyway.'

'Time enough,' said Agnes. Another glance. 'Did you like my soup?'

'It was delicious. What was in it, apart from the leeks and the cream?'

'Just what comes to hand. Mushrooms and such,

and wild herbs of my own recipe.' A few minutes more, while I joined her in picking the fruit over. 'You not finding it too lonesome here, then? You sleep all right?'

'Beautifully, thank you. That dog, Agnes, the one I was complaining about, it seems to have gone. Whose was it?'

'All the folks have dogs hereabouts. Maybe it's got shut in for a change.'

'Let's hope it stays that way. One thing I've been meaning to ask you, have you any idea who took Miss Saxon's pigeons? William told me that someone came with a basket and took them away. Did you see them go?'

This time she nodded. 'Chap that took them works over towards Taggs Farm, two mile past that to Tidworth. Name of Masson, Eddy Masson. It was him got her started, giving her a clutch. Never got keen like him, though, Miss Saxon didn't. She just liked to fill her place with such creatures. Used to take the ones that was no good, and give the best ones over to Eddy Masson again. She said once that when she went, he'd promised to take them. And took them he did, but I don't know if he'd keep them. Why?'

'I just wondered. I suppose the one that's still here was out and flying when the others were picked up. How many did she have?'

'Nine or ten.' She laughed. 'If you don't go to count the rest that used to come in for the food. Wild pigeons, squirrels, the lot. And not just in the attics. I've seen robins and such on the tea-table, and that dratted cat never moving to get rid of them.'

'How dreadful. Now, you'll have a cup of coffee, won't you?'

Over the coffee we talked neutrally. She did not mention the recipe book again.

'Is there anything I can give you from here?' I asked, finally, as she showed no sign of leaving. 'I was just going out into the garden. William has been helping me there, but I haven't got everything identified yet. I'll be dividing the plants soon, if there's anything you've got your eye on.'

But she shook her head, took her leave, and went away down the drive.

As soon as I was sure she had gone I let Rags out into the walled garden for a run, then took him upstairs to the attic. The pigeons – still only three – cooed and rustled and flew up to their perches, where they sat shifting from foot to foot, watching us warily. The dog eyed them, but without interest. All he seemed to want, as yet, was sleep and food, and to feel secure. I left him with food and water and an old blanket, and locked the door as I went out. Then back to the toolshed to remove any trace of his occupancy. Until William came for him I was taking no risks.

After lunch I finished picking over Agnes's brambles. They were good ones, plump and very ripe. A few were too ripe, and these, together with the stalks and leaves, I put aside and threw out on the compost heap by the back gate. The rest of the fruit went into the jelly pan. Just as it came to the simmer I heard a sound at the back door. Not Agnes again, surely? William, come for the dog? Or perhaps – the quick jump and thud of my heart told me who I had been hoping to see. But it was Jessamy, with a bulging carrier bag gripped in hands stained with blackberries.

'Why, Jessamy! Come in. Are those for me? Your mother's just been here, and brought me loads! But how sweet of you.'

He dumped the carrier on the draining-board. He was breathing hard, and his blue eyes, so like his mother's, looked vague and strained. 'Them's no manner of good. Don't 'ee touch 'em, miss.'

'The brambles? Why? I've just picked them over, and they're beauties. What d'you mean?'

The dull, wooden look came down again over his face. He looked away. 'Nothing. Nothing. But don't you be touching they. No manner of good. I picked un these instead. These be healthy berries. And I put elder in with they to keep the witchcraft away. Don't you fret about that, neither. I ast before I took the elderberries down.'

'Asked whom? Your mother?'

'Nay. Nay.' He looked scared. 'Ast her that lives in the tree.'

Oh mercy me, here we go, another touch of old England . . . Aloud I said, gently: 'Well, thank you, Jessamy. Now will you let me take another look at that arm of yours? How does it feel?'

'Better. It be great.'

He pushed back his sleeve and held the arm out. My bandages had gone, and a rag, crumpled but quite clean, had replaced them.

'You've not been to the doctor, then? Who put this on?'

'She did. I had to tell her about th' dog, you see, when I gave her the witch-knot. But she don't know I came here and you was still awake.' He was agitated, trying to reassure me. 'Never told her, miss. I never told her.'

'That's all right,' I said soothingly. 'Don't worry. Just let me take a look, will you?'

The cloth came away with a mass of dark-green pulp. Under it the wound looked fine; clean, pale, healing fast. The bruising had already faded to a dirty yellow, the punctures cleanly scabbed over.

'This really is great, Jessamy! What on earth did she put on it?'

'Leaves. Some she grows out the back. And ointment, Miss Saxon's that was, some she made every summer wi' the same plant. Swore by it, she did.'

'She was right. I won't put anything else on it. Let me bind it up again.'

'Sovereign,' said Jessamy, as his mother had done. He repeated it, like a child pleased to have remembered a lesson. ' "In or out, that's sovereign." That's what she used to say.'

The scent of the stuff was familiar, evocative. Yet how? And when? It smelled of a damp meadow, the edge of a pool, a stream lapsing through green weeds. I could almost hear the rustle of Cousin Geillis's dress, feel her peering over my shoulder as I started to replace the poultice. *Comfrey*, that was it; *called knitbone, bruisewort, consound. The roots boiled in water or wine*

and the decoction drunk heals inward hurts, bruises,
wounds and ulcers of the lung. The roots being outwardly
applied cure fresh wounds or cuts immediately. ('In or out,
that's sovereign.') The recipe – Home Remedy or
Receipt? – unreeled in my mind as if I had made it
a hundred times. *For the ointment, digest the root or*
leaves in hot paraffin wax, strain and allow to cool . . .
And from somewhere faint and far back, a sentence
that ran like a tranquil psalm: *Comfrey joyeth in watery*
ditches, in fat and fruitfull meadowes; they grow all in my
garden.

'Jessamy—' My voice sounded almost as faint and
far away. 'If you need any more of the salve, I'll give
you some. There's plenty in the still-room.'

'Thanks, miss. Thanks.' He rolled his sleeve down.
'And you won't touch they brambles? You didn't drink
the soup. Don't you eat those, neither.'

'How did you—?' I stopped, blinking at him, still
bemused. I said feebly: 'It was delicious. I did thank
your mother.'

A hiss from the stove, and the sweet-acrid smell of
burning fruit recalled me sharply. I hurried to lift the pan
aside. Behind me he said anxiously: 'Don't tell her.'

'What? Oh, the brambles. No, I won't tell her. But
look, if that arm starts to trouble you at all, you must
see a doctor, whatever your mother says. Do you want
your carrier back?'

He shook his head, making for the door. Just before
he went out he paused. 'You will chuck they berries
away, miss? That paddock's broth of hers don't do any
good at all.'

For quite a few seconds after he had gone, I stared after him at the oblong of empty light which was the doorway. Old England, indeed. I did not dare believe my ears. But Jessamy apparently saw himself as being in my debt, and it would do no harm to listen to him.

All right, then, preposterous though it was, Agnes had tried twice to drug my sleep. The first time, with the pie, she had succeeded; hence the nightmare. The second time, with the soup, she had failed. And now a third attempt, with the brambles. Paddock's broth, indeed. Poison? Highly unlikely. Then what? Something to drug me to sleep again while Agnes roamed the house? Looking for what? That book? Again unlikely. Even if that was what she had been searching for earlier, she had no reason now to doubt my promise to let her see it. She had already had the chance to see everywhere except in the still-room, and now I had offered her even that. So why?

I lifted the jelly pan off the stove, and dumped it on the draining-board beside Jessamy's carrier bag. Jessamy meant me well, certainly, but I could not believe he was right about this. Even if for some reason Agnes wanted me to sleep soundly tonight, drugging the brambles would not ensure it. The jelly would, in the normal way, not be used for weeks, even months, and then in small quantities and at times she could not predict. Besides, I might well, as one did, give one or two pots away, or send them (as in fact I had intended) to the parish sale of work.

But – to get back to the first question – why drug me at all? The first time – the pie – was no more than a well-founded suspicion, but the soup seemed to be a fact. 'You didn't drink the soup,' Jessamy had said, and I had wondered how he knew. But I had already had the answer: 'You was still awake.' So they had not intended to come to the house that night, or surely Jessamy would have had to warn her that the drug had not worked. Agnes, I remembered now, had asked me if I had slept well, just as she had asked after that first night.

There was more. She knew about the dog. Jessamy had told her. And though she knew about the bitten arm and the dog's escape, she had not mentioned it when I gave her an obvious lead. The inference was that she had known Rags was in the big house, and had sent Jessamy there herself. Not to feed him; the bowl had been dry and empty. Not to release him, either; the rope had been gnawed and snapped.

So, if he was neither feeding the dog nor letting him go, why had he been sent? And there again I had the answer, in the dog's torn skin, the frantic leap that had snapped the rope and let him escape, the bitten arm, the tuft of hair left in Jessamy's hand. 'I had to tell her about the dog when I gave her the witch-knot.' I had no idea what a witch-knot was; something like an elf-knot, I supposed, a tangled skein of hair; but almost certainly Jessamy had used the term for the tuft which he must have hidden in his pocket when he handed me the soiled cloths to burn.

I left it at that. There was little point in any further guessing. I could ask him next time I saw him, and it was even possible that he might tell me. William had said that he was gentle enough, but he was afraid of his mother, and did as she told him. Well, that fitted. He had been no more than stupid with the dog: if he had thought to take scissors he could have got his witch-knot without the bite, and they would still have the dog.

They would still have the dog. That was the crux. Agnes could do as she liked with her spells, her paddock's broth, her witch-knots and her 'meetings' – covens? – up by the quarry, as long as no living creatures were made to suffer. I would not trouble with poor Jessamy. I would tackle Agnes herself as soon as I saw her, and get the truth out of her.

Perhaps the strangest thing about it all was that, though puzzled and uneasy because I could not see what was happening, I was not frightened. It was as if Thornyhold itself, embattled against evil, was infusing into the nervous, unsure girl I had been, some sort of strength (I hesitated to use the word 'power') which was a shield. The shade, or rather the shining, of Cousin Geillis's presence; doves that brought messages of peace; scented flowers and herbs that hindered witches of their will. *They grow all in my garden.* All that needed to be said, I had said to William: 'I don't know whether such things exist or not, but if they do, trust in God and they can't hurt you.'

I came back out of my thoughts and into the sweet-smelling, normal kitchen. The sunlight glowed in the four pots of jelly. Four was enough. I would tip Agnes's fruit out, and Jessamy's with it. And while I thought about it, I would get some of the comfrey salve, and put it on Rags's tail. If he licked at it, it would do him no harm. In or out, that's sovereign.

I hefted the heavy pan and carried it out to the compost heap. The birds were busy, with no apparent ill effects, on the discarded pickings. Agnes's brambles were surely as innocent as Jessamy's. In any case, sooner than hurt anyone's feelings, I would bury them all out of sight. I emptied the pan, took it back indoors and got the carrier bag and tipped that, too, then went to the toolshed for the spade. I dug a hasty pit beside the compost heap and began to shovel the discarded fruit into it.

I was just finishing the job when I heard the front wicket clash, and moments later William's father appeared round the side of the house, making for the back door. He had raised a hand to knock when he saw me, and turned to greet me.

20

I straightened up to lean on the spade, and pushed the hair back out of my eyes with a blackberry-stained hand.

'Why, hullo! How nice to see you. I – I thought you might come over. Did William ask you to come for the dog?'

'Yes. It made a wonderful excuse.'

'I beg your pardon?'

He smiled at me, and I got the impression that the sun came out and all the birds suddenly burst out singing. I took some sort of control of my besotted thoughts, and said feebly: 'Do come in. I was just finishing here.'

'If I'd come a few minutes earlier, I'd have done that for you. I'm not as good a practical man as William, but I don't mind deputising now and then. Give me the spade and I'll clean it off.'

I surrendered it. 'Did you come through the wood?'

'No, my car's in the drive. Didn't you hear it? From

what William said, I reckoned it would be too far for the poor beast to walk. There. Do you want it put back in the toolshed?' Then, as his eye fell on the empty pile of sacks in the corner, with real anxiety: 'The dog? You weren't burying the dog?'

'No, no! Only some fruit that had to be thrown away. He's fine.'

'Thank goodness for that! I wouldn't have dared go back without him.'

'William didn't come with you, then?'

'No. He's gone on his bicycle to Arnside to see if he can get a collar and lead and some dog food.'

'It's terribly good of you to help out like this. Do you mind? Or rather, do you really not mind? It'll only be for a few days till, well, till things get sorted out here.'

'Look, please don't worry. Of course I don't mind. William told me what happened, and we'll be glad to do what we can. Where is he?'

'Up in the attic. I was afraid they'd – afraid someone might see him if I kept him down here. I was just going up to see him, and put some stuff on that tail. Have you time to come in and have a cup of coffee? Or – heavens, I didn't realise it was that time! – would you like some sherry? I found quite a store in the sideboard.'

'Indeed yes. I know Miss Saxon's sherry. Thank you.'

He seemed to know where it was, too, and the glasses. While I washed my hands and put the jelly pan to rinse he found and brought sherry and glasses into the kitchen. He looked round appreciatively.

'I always liked this house. I'm glad you're letting it stay just the same.'

'I love it. It felt like home from the very start. Shall we fetch Rags down now, and let him get used to you before he's handed over?'

'Good idea. He won't have had much of a chance yet to trust people. Did you find out where he came from?'

'Not yet. I don't really want to, because one thing's certain, I'm not handing him back. He's here to stay. The attic stair's this way, through the back kitchen.'

'I know.'

He followed me through and opened the staircase door for me.

'You know the house pretty well,' I said.

'I came here quite a lot. I was very fond of your cousin.'

As I opened the attic door I was met by a very different dog from the one that William and I had rescued. He came to meet me, and the whole of his tail was wagging. His body was still arched, tucked in over the shrunken belly, but the eyes were different, and they were eyes I knew, eager and loving. I knelt down to greet him, and held him while Mr Dryden made much of him. I left them together while I went to get grain for the birds.

'You knew she kept pigeons, of course? Did you ever come up here?'

'A couple of times.' He was talking gently to the dog, which had tried to follow me, but allowed the man to hold him back. I saw Mr Dryden eyeing the birds as they flew down to the food. 'Three of them?'

'Yes. Did William tell you about the message?'

'Yes, he did. I hope he was meant to? That is – you didn't mean him not to?'

'Oh, no. Was he still worried about it?'

'I don't think so. Puzzled, that's all, but I explained.'

He got to his feet as I dropped the grain scoop back into the crock. Rags came sidling up to me, ears flattened, ready for a caress, then went ahead of us down the first steep flight with a stumble and a rush, and stood waiting on the landing, almost the picture of a dog eager for a promised walk.

'They recover fast, don't they?' said Mr Dryden. 'I don't think you need worry. By the time he comes back to you we'll have him as fit as a fiddle.'

'Can you manage the food, do you think? It's not always easy for the cat, and I've never kept a dog.'

'We're living on a farm, remember. There's plenty. In fact the corn you're feeding to the pigeons was a gift from our hens.'

'Really? I'm grateful yet again. What did you tell William?'

He turned to shut the staircase door. 'What about?'

'The pigeon with the message. You said you "explained" to him.'

'Oh. Well, I should have said, "explained as best I could".'

'Which was?'

'I gather I said much the same as you did. The only way it could have happened is for someone to have taken a bird and released it just after you got here.'

'Yes, but what really worried him was that she wrote

the message herself, and this must have meant that she foresaw her own death.'

'Not necessarily, surely? She may well have pictured herself coming back from hospital, with you ensconced here to share it with her?'

I shook my head. 'She knew. And she knew more than that; she foresaw my father's death as well.' I told him about the dated letter that had been lodged with the will, and what she had said to me that day by the river. 'I told William that even if she did foresee her own death, such things weren't so very uncommon, and in fact I knew Cousin Geillis would have been glad of the knowledge.' I looked at him. 'It would be nice to feel that way, but I'm not sure that I could. Could you?'

He shook his head. 'She was a tougher character than I could ever be. But it fits. It rings true. William accepted it, anyway.'

'Then that's all right. I asked Agnes who took the pigeons and she said it was someone called Masson who lives over your way. Do you know him?'

'Yes, he's Mr Yelland's shepherd. Yelland is the farmer who owns Taggs Farm. It was once two farms, but it was joined into one when he married Bessie Corbett, so now the Yellands live at Black Cocks and I rent the other house.'

'Boscobel.'

He smiled. 'It appealed more than Taggs Farm.'

'And Mr Masson?'

'He has a cottage a couple of miles away, at Tidworth.'

'Do you suppose he could have released that bird on the date she gave him?'

'I suppose he might. If the birds were all there with him, he must have done.'

We were back in the kitchen, and Rags rushed forward to explore Hodge's empty dinner-bowl. Hodge was on the table, washing. He spat once, a token hiss, as the dog came into the room, then went back to his washing.

I laughed. 'No trouble there. Well, the pigeon mystery can wait till I see Mr Masson myself. Do sit down.'

He poured sherry and handed me a glass. 'Does it worry you?'

'Not a bit. Actually, I liked it. It was like her.'

'Have there been other messages?'

'Only one, and that was better still. It came like a blessing from the air.'

He was silent, sensing perhaps that I wanted to say no more. We sat watching while the dog scoured the empty bowl, then came over to us for attention. The cat washed, attending to nobody but himself.

I smoothed the dog's head. 'Do you know of a stone circle hereabouts?'

He looked amused. 'Well, there's Stonehenge.'

'Oh, heavens, I suppose there is! But not as big as that. A little one.'

'Actually, Stonehenge isn't as big as one imagines it from the pictures. Haven't you ever seen it?'

'No. I didn't realise it was so near. I'm from the far north, remember? No, I did wonder if there was a small one, something like the one near Keswick, maybe not far from the quarry? The quarry where we met?'

Even as I said it, something about the phrase

stopped me short, confused. It was a lovers' phrase, and it seemed to go ringing on and on between us.

But he seemed to notice nothing. (And why indeed should he? You're on your own in this, Geillis Ramsey.) He was saying: 'There's nothing like that hereabouts that I know of. Certainly nowhere near Boscobel or Black Cocks. But Stonehenge – you've really never seen it? Would you like to?'

'Love to. Once summer comes again, and I've maybe got myself a car and some petrol to run it on—'

'I have a car, and the tank is full, and the weather is gorgeous right now. How about this afternoon? It's not far.'

'I – why, I'd love to. But – are you sure? What about the book? I thought you were head down in that.'

'For once it can take second place. I was going to ask you today, anyway, if you'd like to go out somewhere; coming for Rags just made the excuse. We can take him home and have a sandwich or something—'

'I could give you something here, if you'd like it. An omelette? Thanks to you, I'm well off for eggs.'

'Thank you, but no. William will be home by now, and he'll be watching the road for you.'

I laughed. 'For Rags, don't you mean?'

'Of course. We'll have a sandwich at Boscobel. Please say yes.'

'Yes. It sounds lovely. Thank you, Mr Dryden. Will you have some more sherry while I go up and get the ointment for Rags, and collect a jacket for myself?'

★　　★　　★

The drive over to Boscobel began almost in silence. I remember the whisper of the car's tyres on the moss of the drive, the dapple of sunlight sliding over us as we purred under the trees, the flash of blue as a jay fled low across the bonnet. My companion did not speak, and whether it was the effect of his close proximity, and the sudden feeling of intimacy given by a closed car, coupled with the too vivid knowledge of my own feelings, I found myself gripped by something of my old, crippling diffidence, and was glad of the dog's presence as a bridge to the silence. Rags seemed nervous of the car at first, and I had to make much of him as I held him down under the dashboard till we were past the lodge.

As the car threaded its way between the twin halves of the lodge I saw the curtains on our right – Agnes's side – twitch ever so slightly, and fall straight again. And on the other side the shadow rocking to and fro, to and fro, in the solitude of the tiny house.

We turned out into the sunlight of the road. Mr Dryden spoke at last. 'They were there.'

'Yes. I saw.'

'Well, you can let him up now. Will he go on the back seat, do you think?'

But when I tried to ease Rags back across the gear-box, he refused to go, so I kept him where he was, on my knee, and sat back as comfortably as I could.

Mr Dryden glanced down. 'Are you all right like that?'

'I'm fine. He doesn't weigh much, poor chap. He'll settle down soon. Do you know, Mr Dryden, it must be years, literally, since I had a run out, like this, just for pleasure. It's wonderful!'

'I'm glad. And do you think you could make it Christopher? Or even Christopher John? That's what I was always called when I was a boy, to distinguish me from my father. Whichever you like. Will you, please?'

'I – yes, thank you. And you know mine.'

The car gathered speed. The hedges streamed by. 'William calls you Gilly. I understand you asked him to. Do you like that, or Geillis?'

I smiled and echoed him. 'Whichever you like.'

'Geillis.' He said it very softly, as if to himself, and a shiver went up my spine. I hugged Rags to me and put my head down to his. 'Do you know,' added Christopher John, 'that it's a real witch's name?'

My head came up with a jerk. 'Good heavens, no! Is it? I used to ask my mother where the name came from, but she never told me. Cousin Geillis's name, I mean. I was called after her.'

'She was your godmother?'

'Sponsor, she called it. She wasn't – at least she made out that she wasn't – on terms with God.'

(The second message: *Welcome to Thornyhold and God bless your sleep*? Who had sent it? Who?)

He was saying something about Edinburgh, and the witch trials there. 'There was a Geillis Duncane. She's mentioned in the *Demonology*. And so, incidentally, is one Agnes Sampson. And I seem to have seen that lamb-like name cropping up elsewhere in the chronicles of witchcraft – as well, that is, as our own Agnes, who works at it with the best of them.'

'And I'll bet she's the prettiest witch in the coven.' I said it lightly, more for something to say than for any other reason.

'Pretty? Is she? I suppose she is.'

Whether it was the indifference of his tone, the absent way he spoke as he steered carefully to overtake a couple of cyclists on that narrow road, but that was the moment at which the scales dropped from my eyes with a thud that I could actually hear, only it was the twisting thud of my heart.

I saw it all – no, not all, but many things that I ought to have seen long before.

Agnes Trapp had not drugged the blackberries. She had picked them because, quite simply, she did not want me to go over to the quarry again, and perhaps go up to Boscobel. And she had deliberately lied to me – or misled me – about Christopher John's wife.

The reason? So bemused and bedazzled had I been that I had not taken into account the fact that other women might be just as responsive to my *homme fatal* as I was. Like an arrow striking home, the simple truth thudded into my brain. Agnes was in love with him, too.

William was waiting, hanging over the gate.

As we approached he swung it wider, and we drove into the yard. I opened my door, and Rags jumped out. For a moment he stood looking doubtfully about him, ready, I think, to be afraid of another strange place, with its new sights and smells. Then the boy called, 'Rags! Rags!' and boy and dog flew together.

We left them and went into the house.

21

We did see Stonehenge. In those days it stood un-
fenced, deserted, small in the middle of the great Plain,
but as one left the road and walked to it across the grass
the stones reared themselves to their awesome height,
and the circle closed round with its own old magic.

This was certainly not the stone circle of my dream.
There were harebells in the grass, and the lichens on
the tall stones were beautiful in the sunlight, green and
amber and furry grey as chinchilla. The breeze in the
long autumn grasses sounded like the ripple of a slow
river. Late though the year was, an occasional bird-call
echoed over the Plain. Above us the sky arched,
enormous, wisps of cloud breaking and forming and
flowing through the blue like the creaming of a quiet
sea.

There was no one else there. We walked slowly
round between the massive menhirs, while Christopher
John told me about the place. Nothing was known, he
said, about its origins or the great men of our pre-

history who had built it, but there was evidence to show where the stones had come from, and this, considering their size and the distances involved, was barely credible. Of course legends had arisen to explain the apparent miracle of the building. It had been erected in a night by Merlin, and King Uther Pendragon lay buried at its centre. The Druids had sacrificed their wretched victims there. Its builders had oriented it towards the rising sun of the summer solstice, and people still came sometimes to pray there, and watch for wonders. It was a calendar, a gigantic time-keeper of the years. It was a thousand-milestone on the path of some sky-haunting dragon . . .

None of it, truth or legend, was needed to enhance the magic of the place. For me, that was there in the clean air and the breeze on the grasses and the singing of happiness.

We had tea at Avebury, at an inn in the very centre of another circle so vast that the whole cannot be seen from any of its stones. Parts of it were lost in the fields round about, and a village with its roads and lanes cut here and there through the ring. We made no attempt to walk round it, but drove home instead by green byways, where Christopher John stopped the car once or twice to let me gather wild flowers and berries 'to draw', I told him. 'I used to do a lot, but I had to let it go rather, and I'd like to start again now that I've got the house straight.'

And all the time, we talked. That fit of shyness had passed as if it had never been, and the earlier ease had come back. I forget now all that we talked about, but at length, on the way home, I began to learn about him. We stopped beside the river bridge over the Arn, with the ruins of the old abbey beyond the trees catching the reddening rays of the sun, and he sat on the parapet and talked while I gathered bryony from the hedgerow, and glossy berries of honeysuckle, and a handful of the exquisite late harebells that look so fragile, but are as tough as wire.

He had served through the war in the Western Desert: he said very little about that, except that he had known Sidney Keyes, the young poet who was killed in 1943, at the age of twenty, and who, had he lived, said Christopher John, would have been one of the greatest of our time.

'In fact is, even so,' he said. 'Do you know his work?'

'I don't think so. I'm afraid I haven't read poetry much at all lately. I used to love Walter de la Mare.'

' "The sweetest singer, and one of the most profound thinkers of our age." ' It sounded like a quotation, which it apparently was. 'He was my wife's favourite,' he said. 'She worked as poetry editor for the Aladdin Press. She and William stayed with her sister in Essex during the war, but she had to go up to London for a meeting, and there was a raid that night. She was killed, while I was sitting quite safely somewhere near Tobruk. William can just remember her.'

He went on then to tell me about her, Cecily, William's mother, dead these six years. He spoke of her with love, but without grief. Six years, and whatever the loss, happiness steals back.

'Or comes suddenly, like the sunrise at Stonehenge,'

he said, looking away through the trees, where the ruins, robbed of the last sunlight, showed ghostly grey. 'Look, there's a spike of wild arum by the abbey gateway. What could you want better than that for colour?'

We got back to Thornyhold at dusk. Christopher John saw me to my door, unlocked it for me, declined to come in, and tripped over Hodge on his way down the path. I heard the car door open and shut.

I snatched Hodge up and kissed him, said: 'Oh, *Hodge!*' and turned to run upstairs. Outside, the car's engine started, idled briefly, was killed. Hodge kicked me furiously and leaped from my arms as Christopher John came rapidly up the path again, carrying the flowers I had picked, and a small parcel wrapped in brown paper.

'You left your flowers. I'm afraid they got a bit squashed, but they might come round.'

'Oh, dear! They were on my lap, and I forgot all about them. They must have slipped off and got trodden on. I'm terribly sorry.'

'Don't be. It was a good thing, as it happens. Reminded me of something I ought to have brought back weeks ago. Miss Saxon asked me to keep it for you. Here it is now, with apologies. And thank you once more for a wonderful day.'

Before I could answer he had sketched a salute, turned and gone. This time the car started with a roar, and went quickly away.

Hodge said something urgent from the baize door, so I pushed it open and carried flowers and package to

the kitchen. Flowers first, into a jug of water. Hodge's
supper next, or there would be no peace at all. Finally,
to unwrap the package.

Whether by witchcraft or not, I knew already what it
would contain. And it did. Lying there on the table
beside the sherry bottle and the jug of wild flowers was
Goody Gostelow's own Home Remedies and Receipts.

Of course I took the book to bed with me, and of course
I sat up half the night, reading it.

Reading, that is, as much of it as I could. Agnes had
been right; the crabbed, spidery hand and the faded ink
made some of the words indecipherable, but a modern
hand – my cousin's – had translated the worst of the
words, and had also pencilled in notes or even correc-
tions to the old recipes.

For that is what they were. If I had expected a book
of magic spells, I was disappointed. It was just what the
title had promised, a book of recipes and home remedies. Some of them Cousin Geillis had obviously
tried and used; here and there she had added notes:
This works well, but use sparingly, half the dose for a child.
Or: *Too violent. Try (indecipherable) instead?* and a
further note: *Yes.* The comfrey salve was there: *For
the ointment, digest the root or leaves in hot paraffin wax,
strain and allow to cool.* I read it with a prickling of the
skin at my own foreknowledge, and a smile at Cousin
Geillis's note: *Culpeper's recipe. Sovereign, inside or out.*
Against another recipe she had written: *It won't grow
here. Italian. Ask CJ.*

The book was not set in order; that is, the recipes

seemed to have been written down as they were acquired, or tried out, so that soups, pies, puddings and so on, were interspersed with pickles and wines, medicines and household cleansers. The medicines, and of course the preserves and wines, used plants, herbs, fungi, mosses, the barks and sap of trees – every imaginable product, not only of the garden, but of the hedgerows and streams and woods.

I read on, and as I read, an idea began to grow, and gradually took hold of me. To begin with I had assumed, with a good deal of misgiving, that I should try to follow in the steps of Lady Sibyl and Cousin Geillis and become, in fact and not merely in jest, the third 'witch' of Thornyhold. But what I had seen of my cousin's library, and the contents of her still-room – her professional life tidied away to make room for something new – had convinced me otherwise. Things had changed. Even to myself I would not acknowledge how, but I knew that the lifetime's study given by my spinster cousin would take more time and dedication than I, with marriage and a young family, was likely to have.

So our minds leap ahead of facts or even probabilities. But mine made the leap, and I knew at last just what I had to do.

The talent you're born with. I would use it, my one real talent, and make drawings of all the plants and fungi, with descriptions, and notes of their habitats, and perhaps some day make an illustrated book of the sovereign remedies and recipes of Thornyhold. Christopher John would advise me. But whether it made a publishable book or not, I would do it for my own pleasure, and in the doing, perhaps, learn how to use in my own way the gentle powers of garden and woodland. I would start tomorrow to make a fair copy of Lady Sibyl's book, and perhaps even try out some of the recipes for myself.

I remembered then that I had promised to let Agnes see the book. That first, then. Tomorrow as ever was I would gather my new courage, take the book down to the lodge, and get answers to the questions I wanted to ask. But no mention, no hint at all, of brambles and the quarry and Boscobel.

Brambles. A thought struck me, and I picked up the book again. I checked through it, curiously. There was no recipe in it for bramble jelly.

Beyond the open window the owl hooted. Overhead some small clawed creature pattered among the remains of the pigeons' grain. Beside me, snuggled deep in the eiderdown, Hodge purred suddenly, then switched off like Christopher John's engine. A big moth flew in, and beat crazily at my bedside light. I reached to switch off and give the creature a chance to get away and back into the cool night.

No recipe for bramble jelly. That had been Agnes's excuse for getting me to look for the book. If she had wanted some of the herbal recipes for herself, surely she would have said so. But there had been those elaborate lies about 'Miss Saxon's jelly was always the best', and the special recipe that must be in this book. And this was certainly the book with the difficult writing that she had not had time or chance to make out.

Conclusion? That the book contained some other recipe that she wanted, but did not want to talk about.

And on the heels of that conclusion, another. That whatever it was, Cousin Geillis had not wanted her to have it. Had perhaps found her examining the book, and so had taken the precaution of lodging it in Christopher John's safe keeping till my arrival.

I switched the light on again. The moth had gone. Hodge half-opened an eye in reproach, then shut it again, stretched luxuriously and sank back into sleep.

I reached to pick up the book. Its cover, never a very strong one, had split with long usage, and the backbone had broken, letting the stitching go. My action in stretching for the bedside lamp had tumbled the book aside, so that it slid, half opened, across my knees, while a loose page slid out free of the rest.

I picked this up and opened the book to replace it, glancing at it half-idly as I did so. It looked and felt different from the rest; a thicker, yellower paper, brownish ink, splotches and blots made perhaps by a quill pen, and in a different, older hand. A recipe supplied by an altogether different person from the virtuous ladies Sibyl Gostelow and Geillis Saxon. A recipe belonging to the book I had expected to find, the only recipe that could claim to be 'real' magic, and pretty certainly the one that our local witch wanted so very badly.

It was called, simply: *The Love Philtre*.

I think that my first emotion was recoil, then, woman for woman, a sort of pity. Afterwards, sharply, and still woman to woman, a flash of uncertainty: am I wrong

about the way he feels for me? And finally, an incred-
ulous: supposing the damned thing works?

I picked up the thick, tatter-edged parchment and
read it through . . .

*The Love Philtre. Take the wings of four bats, nine hairs
from the tail of a newly dead or dying dog, the blood of a
black pigeon, and seethe together with* . . .

I omit the rest. But there already, with no questions
asked or possible to ask, was the answer to another of
my questions.

I sat there in the dark for a long time, trying not to
blame Agnes for what (I told myself) was an unedu-
cated country-woman's attitude to animals. For Agnes,
as for many of her kind brought up in the remoter
countryside of the '40s, all wild creatures were vermin;
a cat was tolerated only as it would kill mice or birds,
even the robin; a dog only as it would work, or act as
guard. She would think nothing of wringing the necks
of my stray pigeons, or drowning the ownerless Hodge,
or keeping the wretched Rags for her witch's cauldron.
I could acquit her of the injury to Rags, inflicted by
Jessamy in his unthinking simplicity, but it was impossible – and, surely, wrong? – to forgive the cruelty
that had tied him up and kept him on starvation rations
for the sake of that repulsive spell . . .

I was trying so hard not to blame Agnes that I found
I was shaking. I told myself that my own deep and even
obsessive love for animals was a personal thing, a
product of my own unhappiness and lack of self-
confidence. Animals were safer, and far kinder, than

people. It was I myself, in my inadequacy, who was abnormal, not the simpler, more extrovert people with their robust attitudes to the natural world.

I thought suddenly of my father's curate, now himself long dead, and what he had done with my rabbit. Presumably he had bred the rabbits for food, and if a child had kept one for love, and subsequently returned it, it would go back into the category of meat. Fair enough. I ate meat myself. The wrong had been done, not to the rabbit, but to the child.

And my mother, with the dog? She had been the product of a tough pioneer society, hacking a living out of the New Zealand bush, where animals were stock or game, and there was no room, in the poverty of a hard-working life, for sentiment. Even the children would be regarded as working tools, and daughters in consequence as less desirable than sons. The wrongs of my childhood, if they were that, could, with this sweating effort of the imagination, be understood, and forgotten . . .

So the obscene love philtre led me, through that long night, to the exorcism of my own miserable spectres, and, finally, to an exhausted kind of peace.

When at last I slept I dreamed, not of stone circles and dying dogs, but of pigeons flying against a high blue sky, and Christopher John smiling and saying: 'Happiness comes back, in the end.'

22

Since this is not a tale of midnight witchcraft, but a simple, a reasonably simple, love story, it is fitting that the final chapters should open on the morning of a glorious day.

Even the early sunshine warming the crisp air, the dew shimmering thick on the grass, and the thin cloud misting the shine of the river, could not disperse the heaviness that lay on me when I awoke. And when I remembered what the day was to bring, I had to hold fast to my courage. Only the thought of Rags, the 'newly dead or dying dog', sustained me. I hurried through the morning's chores, then ran upstairs for the book.

I had no intention of letting Agnes have it until I had had my talk with her and got the truth from her. Even then, I was not going to hand it over with that ghastly recipe still in it. I took the parchment page out and, with no flicker of compunction, set a match to it and washed the charred flakes down the still-room sink. I put the book on a shelf with the rest, locked the door, and went downstairs to prepare, while my resolution held, to go and see Agnes at the lodge.

It is always better to meet the enemy on one's own ground; to choose the position to fight from. I had never been inside the lodge, had not been asked inside on the few occasions when I had stopped there on my way past. I did not want the coming interview to take place in front of Jessamy, and I was certainly not going to talk on Agnes's doorstep. I intended merely to tell her that the coveted book had been found, but that it was fragile and possibly valuable, so that if she wanted to look at it she must do so at Thornyhold, where she would be at liberty to copy out what recipes she wanted.

Afterwards, not to waste this beautiful day, I would go to Tidworth and see Mr Masson, who had taken Cousin Geillis's pigeons, and ask him about the birds that had brought the messages. See if the wild idea I had had about the second message could possibly be right. And (though I tried not to admit it even to myself) see if, as I passed the track that led to Boscobel, I might catch a glimpse of Christopher John.

I cut myself some sandwiches, put one of my pots of bramble jelly in the bicycle basket, and set off down the drive.

At the lodge I met the first check to my brave and cunning plans: Agnes was not at home, and neither, apparently, was Jessamy. There was no answer to my knock.

But as I stooped to put the pot of jelly on the doorstep I heard Jessamy's voice just behind me.

'Why, good morning, miss!'

He had been, not in his own house, but in its twin on the other side of the drive. He had left the door wide. Inside I caught a glimpse of a tiny room, spotlessly neat, with a red checked cloth on a small table, a fireplace glinting with brass, and an old-fashioned rocking-chair where the old lady sat, looking surely twice as old as her years, like a Victorian picture, with an apron over her lap, and a white shawl round her shoulders. She nodded and smiled at me, and waved a hand. I smiled and waved back. Jessamy said: 'Ma's not here, miss. Her's gone out.'

'Do you know where she's gone?'

'Never said.'

'And you didn't see? Did she go up through the woods?'

'Nay. Went towards town.' He pointed in the direction of St Thorn.

'And she didn't say when she'd be back?'

He shook his head. 'Went after breakfast. Never said. Did'ee make the jelly, miss?'

'Yes. It made a lovely batch. Thank you again, Jessamy. I brought a pot for you and your mother. How's the arm?'

'Better. That's healed right up.'

'I'm glad. When your mother comes in, will you tell her that I found the book? Tell her to come up if she wants to see it.'

'A book?' That vague, puzzled look. 'Ma to look at a book?'

'Yes. She'll know what I mean. Just tell her I found the book.' I picked up my bicycle. Gran was waving again, and I responded. 'Tell her I'll be out till about tea-time, but to come up after that if she wants to see it. Thanks, Jessamy. All clear?'

'Aye.' He lowered his voice. ' 'Tain't no use at all you coming in to talk to Gran. She be pleased to see you, that's all.'

'It's all right, I understand. It's nice to see her. She looks very well.'

Another wave, and as I wheeled my bicycle out in the sunny road, I saw the rocking-chair begin its incessant swaying once more.

There was no sign of Christopher John as I passed the mouth of the Boscobel track. Beyond it the road deteriorated into a rutted lane, obviously much used by cattle, which wound between hedges for another mile or so before reaching Tidworth. And there it stopped. Tidworth was remote, a tiny hamlet, with half a dozen cottages huddled round a green where white ducks were enjoying a muddy pond. A pillar-box outside one of the cottages, and some goods for sale in the window, indicated the post office. I left my bicycle at the gate and went in. There was no one in the shop, but the smell of baking bread drifted in from the back room, and the *ting* of the doorbell was answered by a woman who hurried in, wiping flour off her hands on to a large checked apron.

'I'm sorry to bother you when you're busy—' I began.

'That's all right, miss. What can I do for you?'

I hesitated, looking around me, wondering what to buy. There was very little on the shelves; rationing had hit this sort of tiny general shop hard, as people tended to take their coupons into the town where their custom might bring the odd perk with it of unrationed goods. And in a place like Tidworth people would have their own eggs, grow their own vegetables, make their own bread . . . My eye stopped at a stack of unrationed cocoa.

'May I have one of those tins of cocoa, please?'

She reached for the tin, but without taking her eyes off me. She was a tall, bony woman, dressed in black with a rust-coloured cardigan. She had greying hair pulled back into a bun, a strong-looking jaw, and black eyes that took me in with interest, more, with a sharp curiosity that surprised me till I recollected that strangers must only rarely come along this dead-end road.

'Was there anything else? That'll be one and four-pence halfpenny, please . . . Much obliged.'

'There – er – there was something else, actually . . . I'm told that there's a Mr Masson who lives in Tidworth? I wonder if you could tell me which is his house?'

'Eddy Masson? Aye, he's got the end cottage. You passed it, it's the first one you come to on the road. But I doubt you'll not find him there. He'm rarely there except at nights, or Sundays. Works over to Farmer Yelland at Black Cocks.'

Why had I not thought of that myself? To get to Black Cocks you had to go by Boscobel. I smiled at her.

'Thank you very much. I could call there on the way back. But – perhaps Mrs Masson's at home?'

'Not married,' she said, and then, with a disconcerting flicker of amusement, 'not yet.'

'Oh, well,' I said vaguely, 'thank you so much.' I turned with an odd sense of relief towards the door.

Her voice stopped me. 'You staying in these parts, then?'

'Yes. That is, I'm not on holiday. I live here now, at Thornyhold. You must know it? I moved in in September, and I'm still just finding my way about. This is the first time I've been to Tidworth. It's very pretty, but a bit out of the way, isn't it?'

'They say that even the crows ha' to fly out backwards.' She nodded, looking pleased. 'There now! As if I didn't guess who you were as soon as you came into the shop! Miss Ramsey you'll be, as the Widow Trapp works for! Well, miss, I'm glad to know you.'

She pushed up the counter flap and came through, holding out a hand.

Pigeon post, I thought. Pigeon post was nothing to the jungle drums of Westermain. But of course everyone within miles would know of me by this time. Would probably also know me by sight. They would certainly know all that I had done to the house; the 'Widow Trapp' would have seen to that.

The Widow Trapp. And the rival witch lived at Tidworth. The old-fashioned phrase set up an echo that made the guess a certainly. I took her hand. It was dry and bony and surprisingly strong. 'How do you do, Mrs Marget?'

Her delighted reaction held a kind of echo, too. 'There, now, didn't she tell me? Didn't I know the minute I laid eyes on you?'

'Tell you what? Know what?' She didn't answer, but shook her head, the black eyes dancing. She picked the tin of cocoa up and pressed it into my hand. 'You're forgetting this. Yes, I'm Madge Marget, and you'll know my George, I reckon – that's my son. He's the postman, and he was telling me that old Miss Saxon's place looks a fair treat now, and the new young lady was the prettiest sight you'd see between here and Salisbury. So as soon as you come into the shop I says to myself, that's her, I says, with a look of Miss Saxon that there's no mistaking, and a right beauty, too, no offence.'

'No – I – How could there be? Thank you.'

She folded her hands under her apron, and leaned back against the counter, obviously ready for a long chat, but I thanked her again quickly, with some sort of excuse about being in a hurry, and made for the door. As I opened it I found her close behind me. A hand came over my shoulder, pointing.

'That's Eddy Masson's house, a-down there by the stacks. He keeps them there.'

'Keeps what?'

'Those.'

And the finger pointed to where, high over the big elms, a flight of pigeons circled, dipped, and wheeled away in the direction of Boscobel.

23

Mr Masson's cottage stood a little apart from the road, and if I had not been told that he had no wife, I could have guessed it from the generally neglected look of house and garden. The wicket gate was rotting, and hung on one hinge. I pushed through it and picked my way over the weedy cobbles to the door. This stood open, and gave straight on to the living-room, where the remains of breakfast still stood on a table covered with newspaper. A pair of carpet slippers lay where they had been kicked off, in front of the fireless grate.

Another glimpse of bachelor living, and nothing to compare with Christopher John's competence. The only thing they had in common was staring at me from the cold stove. A pie-dish, blue and white, containing the uneaten half of a pie. A pie-dish I recognised. Agnes, it seemed, spread her charities widely.

Purely as a matter of form, I knocked at the door, waited the conventional half-minute for a reply, then,

as if looking for the back door, trod through the weeds
round to the back of the cottage. There, at the foot of
what had once been a garden, stood the pigeon-house.
As I approached it I heard a sound from the air above
me, and looked up, just as the flight of pigeons came
home. Twenty or so, at a guess, grey and white and
black, wheeling against a blue sky. I stood still. They
circled once, twice, a third time lower and more tightly,
then one by one they dropped to the landing-sill of
their house, and went in.

It was apparent that all Mr Masson's spare time and
care was given to the pigeon-house. Though the ex-
terior paint was fading and peeling the woodwork was
sound, and the glass and mesh of the windows looked
almost new. The door, when I tried it, was securely
locked, but by standing on tiptoe I could see through
the wired glass of the front.

Most of the birds were feeding. A few flew up in
momentary alarm as they saw me, but they were used
to being watched, and quickly settled back to their
strutting and pecking. Most of them were grey, like the
first of Thornyhold's messengers, but there were dark
ones among them, and a few of the soft red, and one
pure and lovely white. They were all, as far as I could
see, ringed, but none of them had the distinctive
metallic ring of the carriers.

Not that that need mean anything, I thought, as I
plodded back to the gate. For all I knew they might
wear special rings to carry the tiny rolls of paper. So I
had every excuse in the world for going to Black Cocks
to see Mr Masson, and the best excuse in the world for

passing Boscobel's gate – and maybe calling in to ask how Rags was getting on?

I told myself angrily that I needed no excuse. He had surely made that sufficiently obvious. Was nothing, even the patent liking and admiration – all right, attraction – he had shown for me, going to cure me of the self-effacing instinct built into me by that repressed childhood, the shyness that vanished utterly once I was with him, but which paralysed me from approaching him?

In the end, it didn't matter. There was no sign of him at Boscobel, and his car was not in the yard. Nor could I see William's bicycle. And of course no dog.

I pedalled by, and on to Black Cocks.

The first thing I saw there was Christopher John's car standing just outside the farmyard gate, with William's bicycle leaning against the wall near by. And after all, no courage was required. All that was needed, it seemed, was his nearness. The singing in the air again, the brightness, the lift of the spirit that spelled delight. I propped my bicycle beside William's, and let myself through the gate.

At first glance the yard looked deserted, except for hens scratching and clucking among the spillings from the stacks. There were some pigeons among them, which flew up with a rattle of wings, and I saw that they were wild birds, ring doves that flew high before tilting into a circle and making for the tall elms beyond the farmhouse.

'Hullo? Is anyone there?'

My voice sounded thin and lost in the emptiness of
the yard. The sun beat down on the roofs of the
buildings, and flashed from the car's windscreen.
Cattle lowed somewhere, and I heard a chain clank.
No other answer.

'Christopher John? William?' Then, remembering
where I was: 'Mr Yelland? Mr Masson? Is anyone
around?'

Still no answer, not even a dog barking.

But he was here. I knew it. Knew it even before my
eye was caught by a flight of pigeons that wheeled,
dipped, circled the elms where their wild cousins hid,
then flew away. Grey, rosy-red, and white, the Tidworth flock was out again. The sun glinted on their
tilting wings, making them the snowflake wings of the
crystal. He was here. He must be here. If Cousin Geillis
had been right about me, I knew he was here . . .

Geillis, you lovesick fool, pull yourself together. It
doesn't take a witch to know that! His car's here, isn't
it? All right, then, he and Rags and William, and
probably Masson, too, have gone off with the farmer
somewhere. And at that moment, as if in answer, I
heard a distant barking, and the bleating of sheep, then
a long, sweet whistle, and what sounded like a shout.
The sounds came from some way beyond the buildings
that edged the stackyard.

I gave up, and tried what I should have done for a
start; went to the door of the farmhouse and knocked
there.

At first I thought I had drawn another blank, but just
as I raised my hand to knock again, a girl came

hurrying through from the back premises somewhere, wiping her hands on her apron as she came. 'There now, I thought I heard someone shouting! I was in the dairy, washing up. You bin here long?'

'No. I only knocked once. Are you Mrs Yelland?'

'Nay, then.' She shook black curls, and a dimple showed. 'If you want her, she's over to Taggs Farm giving a hand there. Twice a week, she goes, and she won't be back till tea-time, but you'll be going back that way, likely, and—'

'Actually, it was Mr Masson I wanted a word with. I believe he works here?'

'He does that. I ha'n't seen him today, nor Mr Yelland, not since breakfast. They're over to the thirty-acre, gathering.'

'Gathering?'

'Moving the sheep. You can hear them. But if you'll wait a bit, they'll be in for their dinners. Another half-hour, maybe. There's fences to mend. You like to come in?'

'I – no, I won't, thank you very much. May I wait outside, please? It's such a lovely day.'

'You're welcome, I'm sure. Well, I'd better be getting back to the dinner. 'Bye then.' And she bustled back into the house.

I went slowly through the empty stackyard. During my absence the ring doves had returned, and were busy again among the hens. This time, as they flew up, they went no further than the open door twenty feet or so above, in the barn wall, where they sat on the sill, watching me warily.

It was the sort of half-door, or unglazed window, that opened at floor level on a loft, for loading. And where there was a loft, there would be a way up. I left the baking sun of the stackyard for the gloom of the big barn, and peered round me. Straw was stacked at one end of the barn almost up to the cross-beams, and at the other end right up to the floor of a half-loft. A solid flight of wooden steps led up to this. I climbed the steps to reach a clean boarded floor, lit by a brilliant slant of light from the door. The pigeons had gone. I crossed to the doorway, and knelt there to look out over the roofs of the buildings towards the pastures.

The men were there. In the distance I could make out a small figure that could be William, with a couple of men, and three dogs and a flock of sheep. But not Christopher John. Even at that distance I would have known—

He was not at that distance, nor any distance. As I knelt there, shading my eyes against the sun, I saw him below me, not fifty yards away, just outside the yard gate, with his hand on the door of his car. Then I saw him catch sight of my bicycle. He checked, turned, and cast a look around him.

I drew a breath to call out, then, as if a gentle touch from the air had sealed my mouth, I made no sound. For Christopher John, after that one swift look, whipped open the car door, slid into the driving seat, and almost before my held breath had gone out, was away and out of sight down the track to Boscobel.

24

Now, of course, I could not possibly stop at Boscobel.
But when I passed the gate and allowed myself a swift
look sideways, I could see no sign of his car. I did catch
a glimpse of a woman, whom I took to be Mrs Yelland,
carrying a box into the house, and there was a sack,
perhaps of grain, standing where it had been dumped
on the doorstep. He must have brought supplies from
the farm, and then driven straight on. If he had parked
his car at the back of the house, he would surely have
left the goods there, or carried them in himself. No, it
looked very much as if he had dumped the packages
and made his escape in case I might call on my way
back from the farm.

He needn't have bothered, I thought drearily, as my
bicycle bumped off the track and turned into the side
road. Once he had made it obvious that he wanted to
avoid me, I would be the last person to go near him
even to ask why. In any case, Mrs Yelland's presence
would make it even more impossible for me to stop and

ask him what the matter was. Even when – half a mile later – I realised that he could not have known that I had seen him take that avoiding action at the farm gate, I simply concluded that he had taken the same action at Boscobel in case I should call on my way home. All the old fears and uncertainties came crowding back, to settle, dark and formless, like a weeping cloud. How had I ever dreamed that my love could be returned? That someone like him would ever look my way? What had I said, done, that could have so annoyed – no, disgusted him, that he would not risk meeting me?

My eyes stung, and I lowered my head and pumped away at the pedals as I made myself go back mentally over yesterday, that peaceful and lovely day, when I had thought – been certain – that he loved me. Had the strength of my own feelings deceived me – scared him? But he had said – had looked . . . No, forget that, Geillis. He had been charming and friendly and kind, and I had forgotten to be shy. Perhaps because he had spoken at some length about William, and then about his dead wife, I had read too much into that kindness. So forget it. He had been kind, that was all, to William's friend and lonely neighbour. It came to me like the final, shameful stab of self-betrayal, that he must be used to the effect he had on women. He had seen it working on me, and had decided to draw back.

Then so must I. The next move must come from him. And if it did not come, then it did not come.

The decision, inevitable as it was, came on a flash of pride that steadied my miserably churning thoughts, and brought me back to something near common sense. As the same moment I became aware, for the first time since I had left the Boscobel track, of where I was. I had sailed downhill past the Thornyhold gates without even seeing them, and there at the hill's foot was the River Arn, and the bridge where Christopher John and I had sat yesterday, when all was happiness and the sun was shining.

Well, it was shining today, too. I dismounted at the bridge, took my packet of sandwiches and fruit out of the bicycle basket and, still sustained by that stiffening pride, sat down in the same place on the parapet to eat my lunch.

I suppose, being lovesick, I should have left most of the food, but I was hungry, and enjoyed it, and the warmth and the beauty of the autumn trees, and the flowers in the hedgerow where I had hunted for them yesterday. There was more wild arum growing in the grass beside the crumbling gateposts of the old abbey. The spike I had picked yesterday had been spoiled when I dropped the flowers in the car, so when I had finished eating I wheeled the machine the few yards to the gateway, picked the wild arum and dropped it into the basket with the empty lunch-packet, and turned for home. This was the time for that fresh start that I had promised myself; I would get out my painting tools and begin this very afternoon.

But then I hesitated. Less than ever, after this morning's distress, did I want to tackle Agnes. She was quite capable of hurrying up to Thornyhold as soon as she saw me pass the lodge. I would keep away until I felt more able to face her.

I propped my bicycle by the gateway and went in
through the high hedges to the field where the ruins
stood.

As Mr Hannaker had said, there was nothing much to
see. This was not a national monument, with shaved
turf carpeting a noble nave, and carefully pointed
pillars lining aisles open to the sky. St Thorn had been
a small foundation, but the remains of the church
showed spacious lines, with one pointed arch, still
intact, framing the sky. Nothing was left of the abbey
buildings except, outlined here and there in the grass,
the bases of the old walls, long since plundered for their
stones by the local builders and farmers. The bigger
stones from doorways and pillars – and from graves,
too, by the look of them – had been cleared more
recently, and set back against the hedges, presumably
to make the place into pasture. That cows were pas-
tured here was very obvious.

I picked my way into the remains of the church.
Nettles grew everywhere, and the grass was long and
rank in the shadows, but the centre was grazed clear,
where the worst of the debris of fallen masonry had
been shovelled aside to make way for the cattle. It was
very quiet. No cattle were about, and no birds sang.

I stood in the sunlit nave and looked about me.
Towering above me, with the fragments of its tracery
still clinging, was the arch that could be seen from the
road. The only other remains of any size were the two
massive jambs of the west door, and lesser columns to
either side where the north and south doors had

opened on cloister and garth. Some of the pillars that
had lined the aisles still stood, but most were reduced
to grass-grown stumps. Nothing else, except, near the
west end, a flat slab of stone – what my father would
have called a 'resurrection-defier' – that must once
have marked an important grave. All meaningless now,
deserted, sad. Beyond the broken stones stretched the
empty field. Even the sunlight could bring nothing
back; it was a place for darkness.

It was indeed. I recognised it now. It was not the
same, of course, but it could have been the setting of
my dream. The standing stones of cleared graves and
broken pillars. The empty sky beyond the uprights of
the west door. The flat stone half hidden in the grass.
The feeling of desolation.

'Well, Miss Ramsey, fancy seeing you here!'

I spun round.

Agnes Trapp leaned her bicycle against the gatepost
opposite my own, and came towards me, smiling.

The sight of her banished all other preoccupations
from my mind. So powerfully had I already gone in
imagination through the interview I had planned with
her that I half expected her to tackle me with it straight
away, but all she said was: 'You come in to look at the
old place, then? Pretty, isn't it?'

'Ye-es. Actually, I came to get some flowers and
things. That yellow one growing on the wall is quite rare.'

'Flowers? Han't you plenty in the garden, then?'

'Wild ones. I want to draw them. I used to do quite a
bit of flower painting. I thought I'd like to start again.
Agnes—'

'Yes?'

She had been looking about her as we talked and now turned back to me, with a kind of smiling complacency that made me wonder, suddenly, if she was here by chance, or if the jungle drums – Jessamy or the Widow Marget? – had set her looking for me, to find me here on her own ground. I took a deep breath, and with it a fast hold on my courage. This was certainly not the place I would have chosen, but something told me it was now or never. I left the shadowy precinct of the church, and walked over to where, in sunlight, lay a log; no old unhallowed stone, just a fallen tree, clean and dead. 'I was hoping to see you today.' My voice sounded calm and pleasant. 'I called at your house, but Jessamy told me you'd gone into town. I wanted to tell you that I found the book.'

'You did?' She looked pleased. More than pleased; she sparkled. There was something about her this morning, a shine of pleasure, almost of gaiety, and with it something of that force I had seen in her before. Well, I had not chosen my ground as I would have wished, but this would have to do. I sat down on the fallen log.

'Yes. I was right about it. My cousin had given it to someone for safe keeping because, as we thought, it is actually rather valuable. So you'll understand that I'd rather not let it out of the house, at any rate till I've let some expert or other take a look at it.'

'But she told me I could have it! She—'

'I know. Let me finish. It's there at home, and if you

want to, you can come up and look at it and copy out anything you want. One thing, though—'

'What's that?' Quick, almost defensive.

'There isn't a recipe for bramble jelly in the book.'

'You been through it all, then?' Sharply.

'Not really. I just glanced through for that one, because you'd told me it was special. It's definitely not there.'

I saw the spark of laughter jump to her eyes. She sat down beside me on the tree-trunk, a yard or so away. 'Oh, well, there, I must 'a seen it somewhere else. But there's others I remember I'd be glad to have.'

'Then that's all right.' I smoothed a hand along the stripped tree-trunk. The feel of the warm wood was real and somehow reassuring. 'Any time. Just let me know.'

'Today? After supper?'

'If you like. I'm going home soon.'

A pause. I saw her eyeing me with some curiosity, but, I thought, totally without suspicion or enmity. 'Did you only come here after the flowers?' she asked.

It was my opening. 'Yes, and to look at the old church. But now that I've seen it, I'm a bit puzzled. I feel as if I'd been here before, but I know that's not true.'

Her smile broadened, and she gave a nod of satisfaction. 'I thought you'd feel that way.'

'Why? Agnes, why did you drug me that night, when you left the pie for my supper?'

If she was startled, it was for no more than a second. Then she nodded again, triumphantly. 'I knew it! As soon as I laid eyes on you I said to the others, "She's all right," I said. "She's likely. She'll be one of us, give her time." And I was right. There was no fooling you, was there? You knew straight away.'

'Not straight away. But soon enough. What was in that pie?'

'Nothing to harm, nothing to harm. Just to let you know we were here, and you were welcome.'

I was silent for a moment. 'So that's what it's all been about? You did say once that you'd like to take me along to your meetings. I gather that they're held here?'

She was looking at me with a new expression, in which I thought I could see a touch of awe. 'Do you tell me that you saw this—' she waved a hand – 'these? That first time, without even getting out of your bed?'

'Something very like this place.' I added, slowly: 'And one or two people I'd know again.'

'Then you have got the power! You've got it already! You're one of us, Miss Geillis Ramsey!'

'*No, I'm not. You drugged me, and I had a dream, and it was something like this churchyard, that's all.*' That was what I started to say, but, as if that gentle hand had stopped my lips again, I paused, and said, instead: 'My cousin was here, too. Miss Saxon. She helped me to leave. And next morning a pigeon came in with a message from her, wishing me well.'

The ground was mine now. She went white. 'But that–that cannat be true, miss, it cannat! She wasn't here. She's dead.'

'So?'

'She never was here. She never would come.' She

took a gulp of air. 'And like I told you, the pigeons all went over Eddy Masson's way.'

'So?' I said again. Whether or not I had what Agnes called 'the power', such power as I had found I would exploit while I could. 'You're not suggesting that Mr Masson sent me the message? I'll show it to you when you come to Thornyhold this evening. You know Miss Saxon's writing, I suppose?' I settled myself more comfortably on the log. 'Tell me this, please. When I woke first after that drugged dream, I thought that you and Jessamy were in my bedroom, and I found later that you could have got into the house by the scullery window. Well?'

She was looking down at the grass at her feet. She nodded. 'We didn't do no harm. Jessamy got in that little window and let me in. We came to see if you was all right after the medicine, that's all. You don't always know, the first time.'

Gran. Yes. It fitted.

'And to shut the window up.'

'Ah. That was you.'

A nod. 'You went flying, am I right?'

I said nothing, but she took it for an answer.

'Well, to stop you really going through the window. There's some as do.'

No great shakes as a witch. Poor Gran with her overdose. It seemed I had been lucky. I kept my voice level and hard. 'Did you look through the house while I was asleep?'

'Nay. What was the use? I'd looked already.' She hesitated, then the blue eyes came up, guileless. 'I won't say I didn't look for the key, but I couldn't find it.'

'The still-room key?'

'Aye.'

'And the soup, which I may tell you I didn't drink—'

'You didn't drink that?' She said it, I thought, admiringly. 'How did you know not to drink that?' Then, with a spark of her old self: 'Did another bird come and tell you?'

I laughed, and that disconcerted her, too. 'No. Not that night.' Not to give Jessamy away, I moved back on to half-truths. 'I was awake when that dog cried out, and I saw Jessamy running past the house. Did the dog bite him?'

'Aye. Wouldn't take the food, but broke its rope and bit him—'

'Don't bother, Agnes.' This time I let the anger show. 'I know what happened. Do you think I can't see? I went to the big house in the morning and found where you'd kept the dog. And I called it to me, and it came.'

'That dog? Came? To you?'

'And it will stay with me. Where did you get it?'

'It was straying. Gipsies, likely.' She sounded surly and subdued, and I had no reason to doubt her. 'Would 'a got shot otherwise, a collie straying in sheep land.'

'Well, it's mine now, so you'll let it alone. I won't ask what you were doing with it, because I know that, too. But you'll not touch it again, neither you nor Jessamy. Understand?'

Another nod. She shuffled her feet in the grass.

'Was Jessamy badly bitten? Dog bites can be dangerous.'

'Not bad, and I put the bruisewort on, and the salve your aunty made.'

'Was that the recipe that you wanted from Lady Sibyl's book?'

A look upward at that, slanted and sly. I saw a dimple, and the pretty mouth pursed as if to stop a smile. 'No, miss.'

'Then what?'

'There's one for a cordial from the plums, and I saw some for sweets that your aunty used to make for Gran. She has a real sweet tooth—'

'For *sweets*?'

Unguarded, the syllable was totally disbelieving. She flashed me a look, then smiled, and dipping into the pocket of her coat, brought out a small round box made of wood-shavings, the sort that used to hold Turkish delight at Christmas time. She opened it. Inside, nestling in a white lace paper doily, were small squares of fudge.

'I make a lot,' said Agnes. 'Not just for Mother, for all the sales. Try some. 'Tis my own recipe, this one, and got a prize last time I put it into Arnside Show. Help yourself, miss, do.'

Try some.

Try tackling a known witch on her own ground, and end up sitting with her on a log eating home-made fudge. Try not eating it. I looked at the box, then, helplessly, at Agnes.

'Thanks, but I don't really – I mean, it looks lovely, but I don't care terribly for sweets—'

She laughed merrily. 'So you think it's got something in it that'll set you flying again? Nay, nay, there's nothing here to hurt. Look, I'll eat it myself, to show you.'

She took a piece, popped it into her mouth, crunched, chewed and swallowed. 'There!' She got to her feet and stood in front of me, all at once solemn. 'Miss Ramsey, if I done wrong I'm sorry. We all have our own ways, and I thought the world of your aunty, but I knew, we all knew, that she would never come along with us here. All right. But 'tis no manner of harm we do, just a little fun and a few secrets and something to look forward to come the right times . . . Well, I thought when I saw you, *she* might be different, I thought, and she's likely, so I gave it a try, nothing to hurt nor harm. Never hurt nor harmed yet, except my own mother, and you wouldn't call that harm if you'd 'a known her before . . .'

'Agnes—'

'No, let be a minute. I've not done yet.' She nodded, still solemn, and went on. 'All right, so maybe you don't like what Jess did to the dog, but you know he's not clever, and he knows no better.'

'Would you really have drowned Hodge?'

She stopped, disconcerted. 'Drowned Hodge?'

'Did you try? You couldn't have done it in the well, not after that bird fell in and she put the grating over, but what did you do to him to make him hate you so?'

'There, now, you see!' It was triumph. 'You knew

that, too! But you're wrong about Hodge. He was her cat, and a cat's tricky to mell with. I never did nothing to Hodge. He went, that's all, after she went. Oh, Miss Geillis, Miss Geillis, won't you come with me, just the once, and see?'

'No, I won't. Whatever I know, or have, it's going to stay right inside Thornyhold, and my animals are staying there with me, and nothing of the other sort is to come near us again.'

There was a silence, while we measured one another, eye to eye. My heart was thumping, and my hand, flat on the tree-trunk, was damp. But it was Agnes's gaze that fell.

'Well,' she said at length, on a long breath, as if relinquishing something. 'You mean it, I see that. All right. I promise. Neither hurt nor harm, you and yours.' She took another sweet, and held out the box again. 'So take a piece, miss, and we'll say no more, except that I'm main sorry if there's been any upset.'

What could I do? She was already swallowing. I took a piece of the fudge, and put it in my mouth. It was coffee-flavoured, and very good.

I stood up. 'Well, I'll get home now, I think. I – I'm glad we've had this talk, Agnes, and got things straight. I'll expect you this evening, shall I? Are you going back now?'

'No,' said Agnes. She was standing very straight. The sparkle was a glitter. Her eyes were brilliant, her face rosy. She looked very pretty. 'I'm off to Taggs Farm. Boscobel he calls it. I left some of the sweets there yesterday, while you and he was out sweethearting, and now I'm going over to see them working.'

I stared at her. The barely swallowed sweet stuff made me feel sick.

'What are you talking about?' It was a frightened croak. Some of her wretched drugs . . . sweets . . . see them working. Then, sweets, he doesn't eat them, he'll give them to William. *Too violent. Half the dose for a child.* 'What have you done?'

'Nothing you won't get over! But it's my turn now! I was going to wait till I'd seen the one in her book, the love drink, but after yesterday and the way he looked at you I wasn't waiting any more, and that drink wasn't the only one I knew! So I made the sweets and took them over, and the minute he lays eyes on me, Miss Geillis Ramsey, it's me he'll want, me! And don't you think he'll ever have cause to regret it, neither!'

She shoved the box of sweets back in her pocket and laughed in my face. I said nothing, I must have been staring at her, mouth open, like an idiot, but it was not distress that struck me dumb. She was still talking, flushed and exultant, but I did not hear a word of it.

What she had told me was crazy, it was shocking, but the very shock tore clean through the whirling clouds of the morning's misery, and blew them to shreds. My thoughts settled, clear and still. *Christopher John.* If Agnes was telling the truth, and I thought she was, then nothing I had said or done had alienated or alarmed him. In the sane and daylight world he loved me, and had made it plain. All that had happened this morning was that he had succumbed to some filthy drug of Agnes's concocting, and I knew from my own experience what effect her efforts could have.

So if she had something of witchcraft at her finger-tips, then how much more could I, Geillis of Thorny-hold—?

I stopped short. That way, no. It didn't need the sudden chill of a cloud across the sun, as tangible as that touch from the air, to turn me back from some-thing that I, and Cousin Geillis with her greater powers, had rejected. But the new self-confidence remained. 'In the sane and daylight world.' My own phrase came back to me. It was still that. He and I belonged there, not to the sad and silly world of drugs and nightmare dreams, and in the real world he loved me. He was highly intelligent and articulate; he knew about Agnes; surely, then, all I had to do was tell him all that had happened, and we could talk it out?

Her voice rose, shrill and triumphant. 'Yes, you may well stand there, my lady! So you won't join in with us, oh no! Then you can just stay outside and see what we can do when we want to! And now I'll be on my way!'

'Agnes! Are you out of your mind? Agnes! No, wait, Listen—'

I was shouting at the air. She was already through the gateway, had grabbed her bicycle and mounted. By the time I reached the gateway she was fifty yards away, pedalling furiously. The dappled shadows swal-lowed her pounding form, and she was gone.

I seized my own machine and yanked it out on to the metal. I swear I had no thought of beating her to the encounter, the fairytale meeting that her shaky magic had planned. It was William I was afraid for, with the image of Gran, the echo of Christopher John: *no great shakes as a witch . . .*

But she was pretty competent with a bicycle. As I whirled mine round on the road and made to mount, I saw that both tyres were flat to the ground. And the pump, surprise, surprise, was nowhere to be seen.

A car slid to a stop beside me.

'Is anything wrong?' asked Christopher John.

25

'What on earth's the matter?'

Before I could even speak he was out of the car and I was in his arms. The bicycle went clanging to the ground. Even if I had wanted to I could not have spoken through the kiss. Centuries later, coming to through the things he was saying – 'My dearest girl, my dear, what is it? You look shocked, awful. Have you had an accident on that damned bike of yours?' – I managed to take breath and say, shakily:

'No. No, I'm all right, Christopher John, where's William? Was he to be home for lunch?'

'No. I had to go to St Thorn, but I left him at the farm. Why?'

'Did you get a package this morning, a box of fudge?'

He looked down, surprised. 'Yes. How did you know? Why? What is all this?' Then, quick as if lightning had run between us: 'Oh, my God. Agnes?'

'Yes. You told me, no, William said you hardly ever ate sweets, so I thought you might have given them to him.'

'No, I didn't. I gave the box to Eddy Masson. He was working with the sheep at Black Cocks, and he'd eat sweets all day if he could get them. For heaven's sake, what's in them?'

I do not know what trailing vestige of loyalty, woman to woman, kept me from telling him. But I would not have exposed even a real enemy to the man she longed for and could not have. (Most certainly, now, could not have.) And Agnes, in spite of this last crazy push, was not really an enemy. Standing there in the road, in Christopher John's arms, I could allow myself to see the funny side of it all.

'What are you laughing like that for? A moment ago I thought you were in tears.'

'Nothing. I'm happy. You were saying?'

'I was saying I love you. And what's in those sweets that makes it so urgent . . . and now so funny?'

'I don't know. But there's something. She told me so. She was here, you see, and we had a bit of a scene, and then she dashed off on her bike and I was going after her to warn you and William because I don't trust her recipes, and then I found that.' I gestured towards the fallen bicycle.

'Yes, I saw your tyres. I take it she did that? That's not quite so funny, then. I think we'd better be getting up to Boscobel as quickly as we can.'

A furious hooting drove us apart. He had left his car right in the middle of the road, with a door open and the engine still running. Behind it, pulling up with another flurry of hooting and a squeal of brakes, was the taxi from St Thorn, that knew the way.

Mr Hannaker's face came, grinning, out of the window.

'Look, mate, I don't want to spoil the fun, but I've got a fare to pick up and – oh, it's you, miss. Nice to see you again.'

'And you,' I said weakly. 'How do you do, Mr Hannaker?'

'You settling in all right, then? Getting to know a few folks?' He spoke quite gravely, but I laughed as I went to pick my bicycle up and move it out of his way.

'As you see. You were afraid I'd be lonely.'

The grin came back, broad and cheerful. 'Well, miss, good for you. See you around.'

And as Christopher John moved his car the taxi crawled round it, pipped the horn twice for 'thank you', and vanished round a curve in the road. I pushed my machine in through the gateway and hid it behind the hedge. Then we were away, fast, in the taxi's wake.

Past the lodge gates, and round another bend or two, and the road stretched ahead of us straight and empty, save for the taxi half a mile or so ahead.

'No sign of her,' he said.

'She'll have turned off at the lodge – the short cut through the woods. Can she get there before we do?'

'On that track? Not a hope. But what's the hurry?'

'I suppose there isn't any, really, now. Only I was worrying about William. If Mr Masson gave him some—'

The car surged forward. After a minute he said:
'The stuff was addressed to me. She didn't say why?
No hint at all as to what was in it?'

'None at all.' That, at least, was truthful. 'But she –
she seems to like experimenting with these silly spells or
whatever they are, and she makes mistakes. You know
that; you told me. And – well she tried something on
me, once, and I gathered from what she just told me
that she wasn't too sure of the result. She did say the
sweets were harmless, but William's only a child, so
whatever's in them would be far too strong for him
anyway.'

'Yes. Well, we're nearly there.'

The car turned, a shade too fast, into the side road,
whipped along between the hedges, and at last into
the track that climbed towards the beeches of Boscobel.

As we reached the crest of the hill we saw Agnes,
bumping at great speed along the field path that led
from the quarry to the farm. Bent low, scarlet in the
face, her skirt billowing as she pumped away at the
pedals, she was no longer a figure of menace, but of
bucolic comedy. She did not, mercifully, see Christopher John. All her attention was on the obstruction
that lay between her and the farm gate.

Farmer Yelland's sheep, all hundred and sixty-four
of them, milling and bleating and bobbing around like
froth awash on a millrace, with a couple of collies
weaving and dodging to hold them together right
across Agnes's path. They flowed round the bicycle
and stopped it. There was one with a ragged fleece that

got tangled with one of the pedals, and stuck there, complaining bitterly and very loudly.

Agnes was calling out, but nothing, above the earth-shaking, earsplitting full orchestra of the flock, could be heard. She was not shouting at us. Four-square and thigh deep in his flock, standing stock still and staring at her as if he had never seen her before, was a big man holding a crook. He was chewing.

Agnes dropped her bicycle. It vanished under the tide of sheep. Eddy Masson's crook came down and hauled a lively gimmer out of the way. He waded towards Agnes through the flood of sheep.

'Oh, my God,' I said shakily. 'It works. It really works. And she had some, too.'

'What?' He turned, leaning close to me. 'What did you say? I can't hear a thing in all that racket.'

I smiled at him. The sun was on his hair, showing up the grey. There were wrinkles at the corner of his eyes, and heart-stopping hollows under the cheekbones. I had never seen anyone . . . never felt . . . Here, out of the whole world, was the only man . . .

'Nothing,' I said. 'I was wrong about the sweets. There was nothing in them to hurt. Nothing at all.'

But I still wonder what would have happened if the taxi had come along that road in front of Christopher John.

Bucolic, yes, but an eclogue, a gentle pastoral. The sheep were moving off now, away from the house. Agnes and Mr Masson walked slowly after them, heads close, talking. Neither glanced back. As the car slid up to the Boscobel gate I saw the shepherd's arm go round her.

Christopher John braked, and I got out of the car to open the gate. As he drove through and round to the side of the house William came running from the back yard. He had not seen me. He ran straight to the car.

'Dad! Dad! That pigeon you brought over this morning—'

Christopher John, getting out of the car, caught hold of his son and steadied him. 'Hang on a minute. Did Eddy Masson give you any of those sweets I gave him?'

'What? Not a bite, the greedy pig. Why? But Dad, the pigeon! Mrs Yates put it in the study, but Rags got in and upset the box and it got away. It'll have gone over to Gilly's by now, and you never put the message on it!'

Here Rags, hurtling round the side of the house in William's wake, caught sight of me and came running. William, turning, saw me there. A hand went to his mouth.

Christopher John put an arm out and pulled his son against him. 'It's all right, she's a witch, didn't you know? She knows it all already.'

'*Do* you?' This, wide-eyed, to me.

'Almost all of it,' I said, smiling. 'But I'd like to see the message, if I may?'

Without a word, Christopher John slipped a hand into his breast pocket and took out a tiny, folded piece of paper. I opened and read it. Like the first message, it was in my cousin's hand.

Love is foreseen from the beginning, and outlasts the end.
Goodbye, my dears.

After a while I looked up. 'Of course you know what it says.'

'Yes. She showed me both the messages when she left them with me and told me when to send them. It was her way of blessing you – both of us.' He saw the question in my eyes and nodded. 'Yes, she told me, long before you came here, what would happen. She was comforting me for Cecily's death. She told me that William and I would be healed, and from Thornyhold. As we have been.'

Here William, as Rags leaped to lick his face, caught and held him close. The three of them stood there in the sunlight, hopeful, smiling. Rags's smile was easily the broadest of the three.

It was not possible, standing there facing them, to take it all in, but the paper in my hand made one thing plain. Made fact out of fairytale, and put magic in its place as a natural part of my 'sane and daylight world'. Cousin Geillis had foreseen this long ago, and seen, perhaps, on that day by the River Eden, how her own death would be linked with my coming to life, with the climb of that shy pond-creature out of the dark into the sunlight. It might be that my vision of the doves in the crystal had given her the idea of using her adopted waifs to carry her blessing back to me, and incidentally forge the first bond between Christopher John and myself. The touch of fantasy was typical of the fairy-godmother relationship that she had had with me. Typical, too, was the way I had been left – forced –

to choose my own path through the enchanted woods, where she must have known I would be led to venture.

Christopher John was speaking, something about what had happened at Black Cocks this morning.

'I'd asked Eddy Masson to bring another of the Thornyhold pigeons over to the farm, and I'd just put the box in my car when I saw your bicycle there. That confounded bird was making all sorts of noises, so I drove straight off home with it, and then I had to go to St Thorn to pick up a parcel there. Where were you? I hope you didn't see me running away?'

I shook my head, not in denial, but because I still found it difficult to speak.

'I was planning, in any case, to drive over to Thornyhold tonight,' he said, 'and then send that second message over later on . . . Her blessing, and *envoi*. I was only afraid that I might be assuming rather too much, and a great deal too soon, but I – well, I rather trusted to our talk this evening to put that right.'

Too soon? And I had been afraid it might be too late. Still slightly bemused, I fastened on one phrase he had used. 'That second message, you said? She only left two? But this one today makes three. So where did the other one come from?'

That heart-shaking smile again. 'A blessing from the air. You said so yourself.' He held out his free arm and gathered me to him, with William and Rags still held close to his other side. 'When William rushed home that first day and told me all about you, and later, after I'd met you and talked to you myself . . . Well, I could see that Miss Saxon was perfectly right about the fate I was headed for, but I couldn't let her make all the running, could I?'

I laughed, reached up and kissed him. 'Give William some credit, too! You must know quite well that I'd take anything on just to get him and Silkworm to come and live with me.'

'That's what I was counting on,' said Christopher John.

There is not much more to tell.

We are still at Thornyhold, though our children, William and the two girls, left home long since. None of their families live very far away, so we see them often.

Agnes married Eddy Masson, and went to live at Tidworth. She was, so said the jungle drums, devoted to her husband, and happily occupied her time waging war with the Widow Marget. At any rate, she never tried to come into our lives again, but remained a distant and pleasant neighbour. Gran died soon after the move, peacefully in her sleep, and Jessamy, to everyone's surprise, married a young woman whose good sense and kindness soon pulled him out of his slough of stupidity, and they produced three children who were all healthy, dirty, and perfectly sane, and crowded happily into the two lodges at the Thornyhold gate.

So the witch-story turned into comedy, and the midnight enchantments faded, as they usually do, into the light of common day. The only reason I have told it is because a little while ago I overheard one of my grandchildren, turning the pages of my first illustrated herbal, say to her sister:

'You know, Jill, I sometimes think that Grandmother could have been a witch if she had wanted to.'

Now read on for a taste of Mary Stewart's next tale
of adventure and suspense.

◆

STORMY PETREL

I

I must begin with a coincidence which I would not dare to recount if this were a work of fiction. Coincidences happen daily in 'real life' which would be condemned in a mere story, so writers tend to avoid them. But they happen. Daily, they happen. And on this particular day they – or rather it – happened twice.

I was working in my room, when a knock at the door heralded the entry of four second-year students. Usually I welcome them. They are my job. As English tutor at Haworth College in Cambridge I deal with them every day. But on this sunny afternoon in May, as it happened, I would not have welcomed any intruder, even the gyp with a Recorded Delivery letter announcing a big win on Ernie. I was writing a poem.

They say that after the age of thirty, or marriage, whichever comes first, one can write no more poetry. It is true that after the age of thirty certain poets seem to be incapable of writing much that is worth reading; there are notable exceptions, but they only serve to prove the rule. Actually, I believe that the marriage rule applies only to women, which says something for what marriage is supposed to do for them, but on that sunny Tuesday afternoon neither of the disqualifying conditions applied to me. I was twenty-seven, un-married, heart-whole for the time being, and totally immersed in my work.

Which is why I should have welcomed the students who wanted to talk to me about the poetry of George Darley, which a misguided colleague of mine had included in a series of lectures on the early nineteenth century, and in so doing had worried the more discerning of my students, who were failing to see any merit there. But I had been visited that morning by what was usually at this state of the term a rare inspiration, and was writing a poem of my own. More important than George Darley? At any rate better, which would not be difficult. As a struggling poet in the late twentieth century, I often thought that some early poets achieved publication very easily. But I did not say so to my students. Let them now praise famous men. They do it so rarely that it is good for them.

I said 'Come in,' sat them down, listened and then talked and finally got rid of them and went back to my poem. It had gone. The first stanza lay there on my desk, but the idea, the vision had fled like the dream dispelled by Coleridge's ill-starred person from Porlock. I re-read what I had written, wrestled with the fading vision for a few sweating minutes, then gave up, swore, crumpled the page up, pitched it into the empty fireplace, and said, aloud: 'What I really need is a good old-fashioned ivory tower.'

I pushed my chair back, then crossed to the open window and looked out. The lime trees were glorious in their young green, and, in default of the immemorial elms, the doves were moaning away in them like mad. Birds were singing their heads off everywhere, and from the clematis beside the window came the scent of honey and the murmur of innumerable bees. Tennyson; now there, I thought, was one of the really honourable exceptions to the rule, never failing, never fading even in old age, while I, at twenty-seven, could not even finish a lyric that had seemed, only a short while ago, to be moving inevitably towards the final tonic chord.

Well, so I was not Tennyson. I was probably, come to that, not even George Darley. I laughed at myself, felt better, and settled down on the window-seat in the sun to enjoy what was left of the afternoon. *The Times*, half-read and then abandoned, lay on the seat beside me. As I picked it up to throw it aside a line of small print caught my eye: 'Ivory tower for long or short let. Isolated cottage on small Hebridean island off the coast of Mull. Ideal for writer or artist in search of peace. Most relatively mod cons.' And a box number.

I said, aloud: 'I don't believe it.'

'What don't you believe, Dr Fenemore?'

One of my students had come back, and was hesitating in the open doorway. It was Megan Lloyd, who was the daughter of a Welsh farm worker from somewhere in Dyfed, and who had earned her place in College with a brilliant scholarship. Short, rather thickset, with dark curling hair, dark eyes, and freckles, she looked as if she would be most at home with dogs

and horses, or with bared arms scrubbing a dairy
down, and perhaps she was, but she was also very
intelligent, highly imaginative, and easily my best
student. Some day, with average luck, she would be
a good writer. I remembered that I had promised to
she her about some poems she had written and had
nervously asked me to read. She looked nervous still,
but half amused with it, as she added: 'Surely, *The
Times*? It's not supposed to get things wrong, is it?'

'Oh, Megan, come in. Sorry, was I talking to myself?
It's nothing, I was off on a track of my own for a
moment. Yes, I've got your file here, and yes, I've read
them.' I went back to my desk, picked the folder up,
and gestured her to a chair. She looked back at me
with no expression at all in her face, but her eyes were
twice as big as usual, and I could see the tension in
every muscle. I knew how she felt. Every time your
work is read, you die several deaths for every word,
and poetry is like being flayed alive.

So I went straight to it. 'I liked them. Some of them
very much. And of course some not so much . . .' I
talked on about the poems, while she slowly relaxed
and began to look happy, and even, in the end, cheer-
fully argumentative, which, with Megan, was par for
the course. At length I closed the folder.

'Well, there you are, as far as I'm able to judge.
Whether some of the more, shall I say, advanced judg-
ments of the day will concur is something I can't guess
at, but if you want to try and publish, go ahead and
good luck to you. Whatever happens, you must go on
writing. Is that what you wanted to hear?'

She swallowed, cleared her throat, then nodded without speaking.

I handed her the folder. 'I won't say anything more here and now. I've written fairly detailed notes about some of them. I think it would be better – and we would both find it easier – if you looked at those in your own time? And of course if there's anything you don't understand, or want to argue about, please feel free. All right?'

'Yes. Thank you. Thank you very much for all the trouble. It was just that I – that one doesn't know oneself—'

'Yes, I know.'

She smiled, her face lighted suddenly from within. 'Of course you do. And in return, am I allowed to give *you* some advice?'

'Such as what?' I asked, surprised.

She glanced down at the empty hearth, where the crumpled page had fallen and partly unfurled. It would be obvious even from where she sat that the sheet contained lines of an unfinished poem, disfigured with scoring and the scribbles of frustration.

She repeated, with a fair imitation of my voice, but with a smile that robbed the echo of any sting of impertinence: '"Whatever happens, you must go on writing."' Then suddenly, earnestly: 'I can't read it from here, but I'm sure you shouldn't throw it away. Give it another go, won't you, Dr Fenemore? I loved that last one of yours in the *Journal*. Please.'

After a pause that seemed endless, I said, rather awkwardly: 'Well, thank you. But in term time . . . One can't choose one's times, you see.'

'Can one ever?'

'I suppose not.'

'I'm sorry, I shouldn't have said that.' Suddenly embarrassed, she gathered her things together and started to get to her feet. 'None of my business, but I couldn't help seeing. Sorry.'

More to put her at her ease again than for any other reason I picked up *The Times* and showed it to her.

'I was trying, you see. A Hebridean island – it does sound like a place where one could work in peace, and they have actually called it an "ivory tower". There, I've ringed it.'

She read the advertisement aloud, then looked up, bright-eyed. 'Mull? An island off Mull? You've answered this?'

'I was thinking of it.'

'Well, isn't that something? Ann Tracy and I are going to Mull this summer. Two weeks. She's fixing it up, I've never been, but her people used to spend holidays up there, and she says it can be fabulous, weather and midges permitting. What a coincidence! It sounds just the thing – like fate, really, after what you were saying. You will answer it, won't you?'

'It looks as if I'd better, doesn't it?' I said. 'I'll write this very evening.'

But fate had not quite finished with me. That evening my brother Crispin telephoned me.

Crispin is a doctor, a partner in a four-man practice in Petersfield in Hampshire. He is six years older than I am, married, with two children away at school.

He would have preferred, I knew, to keep them at home, but Ruth, his wife, had overruled him in that, as she did in quite a few other matters. Not that Crispin was a weak man, but he was a very busy one, and had to be content to leave the management of their joint lives largely to his highly capable wife. They were tolerably happy together, as marriages seem to go, a happiness achieved partly by agreeing to differ.

One thing they different about was holidays. Ruth loved travel, cities, shops, theatres, beach resorts. Crispin, when on leave from his demanding routine, craved for peace and open spaces. He, like me, loved Scotland, and made for it whenever he got the chance. There he walked and fished and took photographs which later, when he found time, he processed himself in a friend's darkroom. Over the years he had acquired real skill in his hobby, and had exhibited some of his studies of Scottish scenery and wildlife; his real passion was bird photography, and through the years he had amassed a remarkable collection of pictures. Some of these had been published in periodicals like *Country Life* and the wildlife journals, but the best had never been shown. I knew he had a private hope that some day he might make a book with them. When our vacations coincided, we often holidayed together, content in our respective solitudes.

So when he rang up that evening to tell me he was taking a fortnight's leave towards the end of June and what about a trip north as soon as term ended, I did feel as if the fates themselves had taken a hand.

'I'd been planning that very thing.' I told him

about the advertisement, and he was enthusiastic. I let him talk on about harriers and divers and skuas and all the rare and marvellous birds that would no doubt be waiting around to be photographed, and then put in the usual cautious query: 'And Ruth?'

'Actually, no, not this time.' The usual casual answer. 'She doesn't like the Highlands, you know that, and she's got rather a lot on just at present. She's planning to take a holiday abroad later on, after John and Julie go back to school. But if you can get this place . . . It could be really good. Most of the young birds will still be at the nest, and if the weather lets up, we might get across to the Treshnish Isles as well. Look, Rose, why not? It sounds great. Why don't you go right ahead and get the details, and then we'll be in touch again?'

And so it was arranged. I wrote that night to the box number.

And got my ivory tower.

2

The Isle of Moila is the first stop past Tobermory. It
is not a large island, perhaps nine miles by five, with
formidable cliffs to the north-west that face the weather
rather like the prow of a ship. From the steep sheep-
bitten turf at the head of these cliffs the land slopes
gently down towards a glen where the island's only
sizeable river runs seawards out of a loch cupped in
a shallow basin among low hills. Presumably the loch
– lochan, rather, for it is not large – is fed by springs
eternally replenished by the rain, for nothing flows
into it except small burns seeping through rush and
bog myrtle, which spread after storms into sodden
quagmires of moss. But the outflow is perennially full,
white water pouring down to where the moor cleaves
open and lets it fall to the sea.

The island's coast is mainly rocky, but, except for
the northerly crags, the coastal cliffs are low, thrusting
out here and there into the sea to enclose small curved
beaches. Most of these are shingle beaches, but those
facing west are sandy, the white shell sand of the
Atlantic shore, backed by the machair, that wonderful
wild grassland of the west coast, which in May and

June is filled with flowers and all the nesting birds that any photographer could wish for.

When I first saw Moila it was on a beautiful day in the last week of June. My term had ended a few days before the start of Crispin's leave, so we had agreed to travel up separately, and meet on Moila itself. The island ferry, as I had discovered, sailed three times a week, on Mondays, Wednesdays and Saturdays; it went from Oban to Tobermory on the Isle of Mull, and then called at Moila on its way to Coll and Tiree. I had also discovered that there would be little, if any, use for a car on Moila, so both my brother and I had arranged to travel up by train.

It was a pleasant journey. I took the night train for Fort William, which stops at Crianlarich at seven in the morning. With a three-hour wait there, I ate a large breakfast, did a quarter of the day's crossword, then boarded the little local train that runs through Glen Lochy and past the northern end of Loch Awe, to finish at Oban on the west coast. The ferry for the outer isles was due to leave at six on the following morning, so I checked into the waterfront hotel where I had booked, then spent the day exploring Oban, and went to bed early. At half past five next morning I boarded the ferry, and was on the final stage of my journey.

The sea was calm, and Oban, caught in the clear light of a summer morning, looked charming and toylike, as we sailed sedately out between the islets and castle-crowned rocks, with seabirds drifting in our wake, and everywhere, even over the smell of salt and

wind, the scents of summer. Idyllic. Just the setting
for an ivory tower.

Or so I still hoped. Nobody I had spoken to in the
train, or on the ferry, had ever visited Moila, which
must support, so I was told by one slow-spoken
Highlander, no more than thirty folk in all.

'So you'll be right back to nature, and let us hope
that the natives are friendly.' The twinkle in his eye
was reassuring, but when we tied up at Tobermory
and the purser pointed out to sea where a group of
small rocks (or so it seemed) showed strung out on
the horizon like a mother duck with her ducklings
after her, I felt a cowardly twinge, and found myself
wondering what the 'relatively mod cons' could be.

'Yon big island, see? That's Moila,' said my guide.

'And the others?'

'Och, they've all got names, but I could not tell you
what they are. There's no folk there, only the birds.'

'Can you get to them?'

'Oh, aye, with a bit of luck, on a fine day. Parties
do go out, folks with cameras to film the birds. You're
one of these bird watchers, are you?'

'Not really. But my brother's very keen. He's coming
to join me later this week. Do you know if we'll be
able to hire a boat in Moila?'

But here he had to leave me to attend to stores
which were being brought on board, and some twenty
minutes later I could see the place for myself.

The ferry was not big, but she dwarfed the harbour
– she had to stand off from the jetty and land us by

boat – and indeed the village. As far as I could see,
there were some eight or nine cottages strung out on
a narrow road which circled the bay. The building
nearest the jetty was the post office-cum-shop. A
home-made notice informed me that it was kept by
M. McDougall, who also did bed and breakfasts. Some
fifty yards away was a white-washed building
surrounded by a stretch of asphalt; the village school,
I was to discover, where on alternate Sundays the
minister from Tobermory came over to hold a service.
A narrow river, little more than a stream, lapsed gently
over its stones past the post office. It was spanned
by a narrow humpbacked bridge of the picturesque
variety that is guaranteed to damage any car that uses
it. But, as I had been warned, there were no cars.
One battered Land Rover stood outside the post
office, and leaning against the schoolhouse wall were
a couple of bicycles. No other forms of transport.
Nor, as far as I could see, did the road continue
beyond the end of the village.

And my cottage, I had been informed, lay at the
other side of the island.

Well, I had asked for it. I left my cases parked on
the quay, and made my way into the post office.

Since the thrice-weekly visit of the ferry brought
all the island's mail and supplies, and the post office
was very small, the place was crowded, and the postmistress, busily sorting through a pile of mail and
newspapers, while exchanging two days' news in
Gaelic with the ferry's master, had no glance to spare
for me. The little shop had been arranged as what

I have seen described as a mini-hypermarket, so I found a basket and busied myself with collecting what supplies I thought I might need for the next couple of days. I was called to myself by the echoing hoot of the ferry's siren, to find that the shop had emptied of its crowd, and the postmistress, taking off her spectacles, was hurrying round to the store counter to look after the stranger.

'You'll be the young lady for Camus na Dobhrain? Miss Fenemore, was it?'

She was a thinnish woman of perhaps fifty, with greying hair carefully arranged, and very blue eyes. She wore a flowered smock, and her spectacles hung round her neck on a cord. She had the beautiful skin of the islands, with hardly a wrinkle, except near the eyes, where the smile lines puckered the corners. She was not smiling now, but her look was full of a benevolent curiosity, and the soft island voice, with the lilt of the Gaelic moving through it like a gentle seaswell, warmed me as palpably as if the sun had come into the dim and cluttered little shop.

'Yes, I'm Rose Fenemore. And you are Mrs McDougall? How do you do?' We shook hands. 'And yes, I'm for the cottage that the Harris Agency advertised. Is that the one? I don't understand Gaelic, I'm afraid.'

'And how should you? Yes, indeed, that is the one. The English for it is "Otters' Bay". It is the only place on Moila that is to let. We're not just a metropolis, as you see.' She smiled, busying herself with my purchases as she spoke. 'You'll not have been here before, then? Well, if the weather stays fine you'll find plenty of nice walks, and I'm told that the house at Otters' Bay is comfortable enough these days. But lonely. You are by yourself, are you?'

'Till Wednesday, at least. My brother's hoping to come then.' I gave her all she wanted to know. I was part of the week's news, after all. 'He's a doctor, from Hampshire. He couldn't get away when I did, so I came up on my own. Does the Wednesday ferry come in at the same time?'

'It does. You have not put any firelighters in. You will find it is much easier to get your fire going with one of those. Are you used to a peat fire?'

'No, but I'm hoping I can learn. Mrs McDougall, how do I get from here to the cottage? I'm told it's about two miles. I can easily walk to do shopping and so on, but I've got a couple of suitcases here now, and I certainly can't manage those.'

'No worry about that. I saw your cases there, and Archie McLaren will have them into the Land Rover by this time. So will you perhaps be wanting a couple of bags, say, of coal to help with the fire? The house will be dry enough; there was a couple in it through the middle of May, and we have had good weather, but you would be better to stock up now for what next week might bring.'

'Yes, of course. Thank you very much. Two bags of coal, then, please, and the firelighters, and – yes, I think I've remembered everything else. Oh, about milk and bread. Can one only get it fresh when the ferry comes over?'

'We have fresh milk here from the farm, but you would be better to take some of the long-life with you. It's a long walk from Otters' Bay in the bad weather. Here it is. Two cartons, and it will keep a long time, even with no fridge. I don't know if you have one over there . . . The bread comes with the boat. Will I keep you a loaf on Wednesday? And another at the weekend, or two then, perhaps? Mostly we make our own if we want it fresh. There, is that everything?'

'I think so, thank you. How much is that, Mrs McDougall?'

She told me, and I paid her. A young man, dark, short, burly, in a navy guernsey and jeans and gumboots, came in and lifted the coal bags into the Land Rover beside my cases. I picked up the carrier bag where the postmistress had packed my groceries.

'I don't imagine there's a telephone at the cottage, is there?'

'There is not. There is one here, and one at the House, and that is all there are. And the one at the House is cut off since the old lady died.'

'The House?' Somehow, the way she said it gave it a capital letter.

'The big house. It's not far from you, half a mile along the shore, maybe. Taigh na Tuir, they call it. That means House of the Tower. There is a small island off the coast just there, with the remains of a broch on it. I suppose that is the tower that the House was named for. It was built as a shooting lodge in the old days, and then the Hamiltons bought it, and lived there most summers, but old Mrs Hamilton, she was the last of them, died this February, so it's empty now, and likely to stay so.' She smiled. 'It's not everyone wants the kind of peace and quiet we have on Moila.'

'I can imagine. Well, I'm all set to enjoy it, anyway. And I don't really want a phone, except to make sure about my brother's coming. So I'll walk over here tomorrow and telephone him, if I may. What time do you shut?'

'Half past five, but if you want the telephone, then come to the house door. No, it's no trouble, it's what everyone does, and the cheap calls are after six anyway. Just you come. That's it, then.' She picked up the second carrier bag and saw me to the door with it. 'Archie will see you into the house, and if there's anything more that you need, you will let him know. And I'll look for you maybe tomorrow. Goodbye. Look after the lady, now, Archie.'

Archie was understood to say that he would. I got in beside him, and we set off. The Land Rover had seen better days, and once we had left the village street and taken to the track – it was little more – that wound up from the village towards the moorland, conversation was difficult. After one or two tries, met by a nod or a non-committal noise from Archie, I gave up, and looked about me.

I suppose that there are very few places on Moila from which one cannot see the sea. The track, rough and strewn with stones, climbed, at first gently, through sheep-cropped turf bristling with reeds and thistles and islanded with stretches of bracken. Once we were out of sight of the village there were no trees except, here and there, thorns dragged sideways by the wind and shorn close by the weather. The track grew steeper, and twisted. Now to either hand was heather, at this season still dark and flowerless, except where patches of the early bell heather splashed their vivid purple across grey rock. The whins, those perpetual wonders, were blazing gold, and everywhere over the stretches of grass between the bracken spread the tiny white and yellow flowers of lady's bedstraw and tormentil. The very lichen patching the grey rocks was bright mustard-gold, like flowers. Away to the right I saw the flat gleam of the loch.

Nothing could be heard above the noise of the engine, but I saw a lark spring skywards out of the heather, and another, a few minutes later, sink to its rest. A pair of grey-backed crows – hooded crows – flew across the track, and then, as the Land Rover topped the rise and started down into a narrowing glen, a buzzard soared up in leisurely circles, to be lost over the crest of the moor.

Then we were running gently downhill beside a burn, towards the distant gleam of the sea. Here, in the shelter that the glen gave from the Atlantic gales, the trees crowded close, and reasonably tall. Oaks, mostly, but there were beeches and ash trees, with birch and hazel everywhere, tangled with brambles and wild honeysuckle. Along the edge of the burn were thickets of alder and hawthorn standing knee-deep in foxgloves.

The track levelled out, the glen widened, and there below us was the bay.

Otters' Bay was very small, a pebbled crescent backed by a storm beach of smooth boulders. Thick black curves of dry seaweed marked the reach of the tides. To our left a high cliff cut off the view, and to the right a lowish headland jutted well out into the sea. Narrowing my eyes against the Atlantic glitter I could see the line of a path that climbed from the bay and on over the headland to the west. And beyond the crest of the headland, hazy with distance, the shape of a hill, smooth and symmetrical, like a drawn-up knee.

Then the Land Rover came to a halt beside a rough jetty made of stacked boulders tied down with fencing wire, and there, backed against the cliff a short way above us, was the cottage.